Triumph 1300
1300 TC & 1500

Covers all front wheel drive
models 1965 to 1973

Owner's Handbook/Servicing
Guide

by Marcus S Daniels

46047782⅄

Acknowledgements

Thanks are due to Gil Kirk whose car was used for many of the photographs in this handbook.

Advice on lubrication was supplied by Castrol Limited, and on spark plug conditions by the Champion Sparking Plug Company.

Special thanks are due to all those people at Sparkford who helped in the production of this handbook, including Brian Horsfall who carried out the workshop procedures, Les Brazier the photographer, John Austin who edited the text and Lee Saunders who planned the layout of each page.

A book in the Haynes Owner's Handbook/Servicing Guide Series

© Haynes Publishing Group 1979

Published and printed by the Haynes Publishing Group, Sparkford, Yeovil, Somerset BA22 7JJ.

ISBN 0 85696 389 5

Contents

Triumph 1500

4

What's in it for You?

Whether you've bought this book yourself or had it given to you, the idea was probably the same in either case – to help you get the best out of your Triumph 1300 or 1500 saloon, and perhaps to make your motoring a bit less of a drain on your hard-earned cash at the same time.

Garage labour charges can easily be several times your own hourly rate of pay, and usually form the main part of your servicing bill; we'll help you avoid them by carrying out the routine services yourself. Even if you *don't* want to do the regular servicing, and prefer to leave it to your Leyland dealer, there are some things you should check regularly just to make sure that your car's not a danger to you or to anyone else on the road; we tell you what they are.

If you're about to start doing your own servicing (whether to cut costs or to be sure that it's done properly) we think you'll find the procedures described give an easy-to-follow introduction to what can be a very satisfying way of spending a few hours of your spare time.

We've included some tips that should save you some money when buying replacement parts and even while you're driving; there's a chapter on cleaning and renovating your car, and another on fitting accessories.

Apart from the things every 1300/1500 owner needs to know to deal with mishaps like a puncture or a broken headlamp, we've put together some Troubleshooter Charts to cover the more likely of the problems that can crop up with even the most carefully maintained car sooner or later.

If the bug gets you, and you're keen to tackle some of the more advanced repair jobs on your car, then you'll need our Owner's Workshop Manual for the Triumph 1300 and 1500 (No. 054) which gives a step-by-step guide to all the repair and overhaul tasks on these cars, with plenty of illustrations to make things even clearer.

Triumph 1300TC

The Triumph 1300/1500 Family

The Triumph 1300 saloon car was first announced in October 1965 although it did not come on the market until early in 1966. The body style is basically a shrunken version of the Triumph 2000 with all the luxury features of its big brother.

Mechanically, however, it is quite different from the 2000 model. It has front wheel drive with the engine, gearbox and final drive all located beneath the bonnet as an integral unit. The engine is basically the same as that of the Triumph Spitfire and is fitted in the fore and aft position with the transmission assembly bolted beneath it. Two short driveshafts extend from the final drive unit to the front wheels.

Independent front and rear suspension is used with disc brakes on the front wheels and drum brakes on the rear. All models have four doors with a respectable sized boot and lavish interior equipment.

Several special features are included which are normally only seen on larger, more expensive cars — adjustable steering column, ventilated upholstery, recessed window winders and door handles and a unique 'all in one dial' warning light cluster.

The Triumph 1300 TC appeared in October 1967 and was produced alongside the 1300. This was simply an increased performance version of the same saloon, distinguished by 'TC' badges on the rear and front side wings, having twin carburettors, a raised compression ratio, a modified crankshaft forging a new camshaft and servo assisted braking system.

The Triumph 1500 was introduced in August 1970 and retained the front wheel drive layout. The rear suspension however is not the independent type and comprises a rigid beam axle. The 1500 model is distinguishable by its longer bonnet, extended boot and a divided radiator grille with a 1500 badge in the centre.

The following table lists the various modifications that were incorporated during the production of the 1300 and 1500 models. All the specification details are given in *Vital Statistics* which you'll find further on in this Handbook.

Triumph 1300

September 1965	Model introduced, styled as a smaller version of the Triumph 2000, but with front wheel drive arrangement
October 1967	1300 TC model introduced — same design as the standard 1300 but with twin SU carburettors, higher compression ratio and servo assisted disc brakes
June 1970	Discontinued to be superseded by the Triumph 1500 model

Triumph 1500

August 1970	Introduced to replace the 1300 model. Similar body style but slightly larger. Mechanically very similar but larger engine and rigid beam rear axle. Twin headlights, alternator and servo assisted disc brakes fitted as standard
May 1971	Static type seat belts fitted as standard
January 1972	Heated rear window fitted as standard
August 1973	Discontinued to be replaced by the 1500 TC which has a completely different mechanical layout

Road Test Data taken from *Autocar*

The figures published here are extracts from *Autocar* magazine road tests.

Fuel consumption: The mpg figure is the overall consumption figure for their test period, including performance testing. Many owners will achieve significantly better consumption figures. The formula on the right provides a guide ('**mpg**' refers to the quoted overall test figure).

	1300	1300 TC	1500
Maximum speed (mph)	84	93	85
Overall fuel consumption (mpg)	28	30	27
Fuel consumption (mpg) at constant:			
30 mph	45	N/A	50
50 mph	34	N/A	38
70 mph	23	N/A	27
Range on full fuel tank (miles)	330	354	338
Acceleration (seconds):			
0–30 mph	5·3	5·0	5·0
0–40 mph	8·4	7·5	7·6
0–50 mph	12·8	10·5	11·7
0–60 mph	19·0	15·9	17·1
0–70 mph	29·6	22·4	25·9
Standing start $\frac{1}{4}$ mile	21·3	20·2	20·7
40–60 mph in normal top gear	12·5	13·0	11·8

Driving style	Driving conditions		
	severe	average	easy
Hard	−10%	**mpg**	+10%
Average	**mpg**	+10%	+20%
Gentle	+10%	+20%	+30%

In the Driving Seat

In this chapter we're going to take a detailed look at some of the instruments and gadgets you'll see displayed in front of you when you sit in the driver's seat of your Triumph. We're going to assume that you're fairly well versed in the actual technique of driving, because this chapter's not really intended to be a substitute for a driving lesson, but we'll consider a few instruments and systems of which perhaps the average motorist doesn't understand the full implications involved. If you've just recently bought your Triumph, it will probably be a good idea to read this chapter while you're sitting in the driving seat, so that you can locate the various items and familiarise yourself with them.

The accompanying illustrations show the layouts of the various models and, in general, these are self-explanatory, but the following points may be helpful to those who have recently taken up motoring or who wish to refresh their knowledge of the Triumph layout.

Warning lights

Ignition warning light

The ignition warning light's located together with other warning lights on the central warning cluster as shown on the accompanying illustrations. This light serves a dual purpose; first it tells the driver that the ignition circuit's switched on, even though the engine may not be running, and secondly it shows that the battery's receiving a charge from the alternator or dynamo (check in *Vital Statistics* which unit your car has fitted). If the engine's stopped, the warning light should glow when the ignition's switched on. When the engine's started and is ticking over at a slow speed, the light will still glow, but as soon as the engine speed rises above a fast idle it should go out completely.

The most important thing to remember with this warning light is that, if it comes on while you're driving, you should immediately slow down and find a safe parking place. Switch off the engine, open the bonnet, and do a spot of investigating. The

implications are that the charging system has failed, but this may be due to a broken fan belt resulting in the alternator or dynamo not running; if you continue driving the car with the fan belt missing, you could easily end up with a very hot engine which could be ruined. If you find that the fan belt's still intact and correctly tensioned, then you've got an electrical fault which will need urgent attention.

Oil pressure warning light

The light is also located on the central warning cluster and warns the driver of a sudden drop in engine oil pressure. Oil pressure in the engine ensures that all the moving parts are adequately supplied with enough oil to keep them operating smoothly, so a lack of oil pressure can only lead to disaster as far as the engine's concerned, and to seizure of the moving parts. For this reason you should always *switch off the engine immediately* should this light come on when you're driving. Check the oil level, and if this is OK, you should get the nearest garage to sort the problem out; it may be a simple matter like a faulty oil pressure switch, but on the other hand you may have a bigger problem so don't drive the car.

By the way, the light will come on when you first switch the ignition on as there will be no pressure in the stationary engine but, as soon as the engine starts, the light should go out within a second or two. Try to get out of the habit of revving your engine

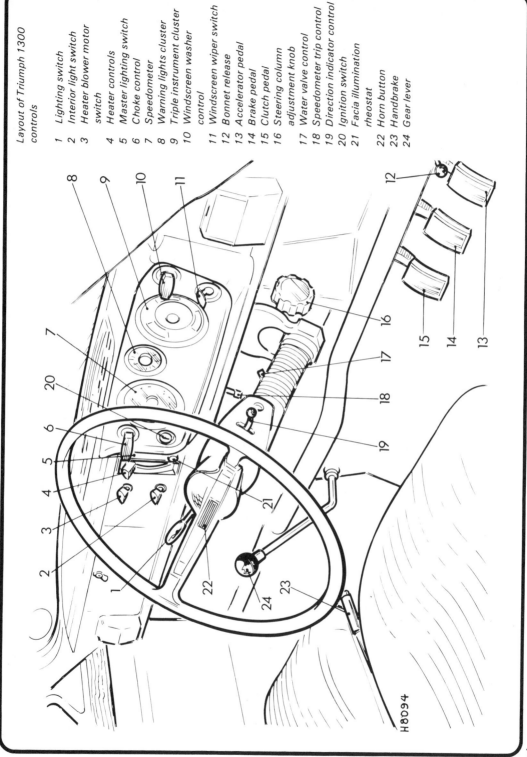

Layout of Triumph 1300 controls

1 Lighting switch
2 Interior light switch
3 Heater blower motor switch
4 Heater controls
5 Master lighting switch
6 Choke control
7 Speedometer
8 Warning lights cluster
9 Triple instrument cluster
10 Windscreen washer control
11 Windscreen wiper switch
12 Bonnet release
13 Accelerator pedal
14 Brake pedal
15 Clutch pedal
16 Steering column adjustment knob
17 Water valve control
18 Speedometer trip control
19 Direction indicator control
20 Ignition switch
21 Facia illumination rheostat
22 Horn button
23 Handbrake
24 Gear lever

H8D94

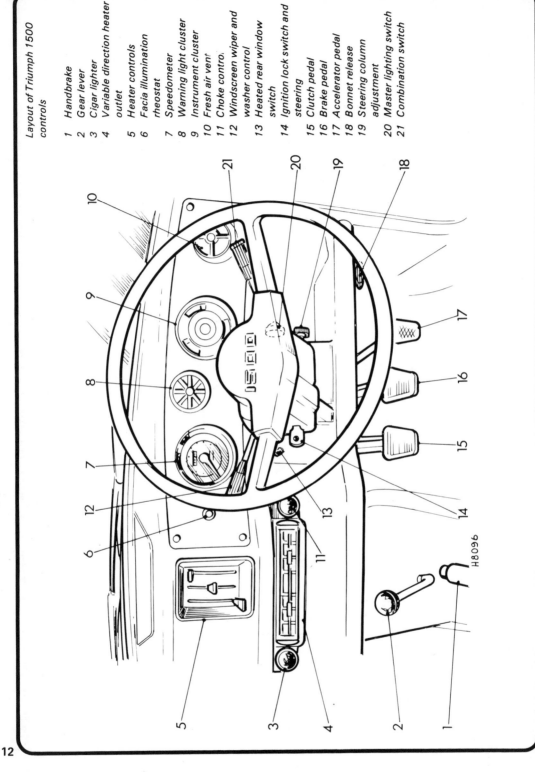

Layout of Triumph 1500 controls

1 Handbrake
2 Gear lever
3 Cigar lighter
4 Variable direction heater outlet
5 Heater controls
6 Facia illumination rheostat
7 Speedometer
8 Warning light cluster
9 Instrument cluster
10 Fresh air vent
11 Choke control
12 Windscreen wiper and washer control
13 Heated rear window switch
14 Ignition lock switch and steering
15 Clutch pedal
16 Brake pedal
17 Accelerator pedal
18 Bonnet release
19 Steering column adjustment
20 Master lighting switch
21 Combination switch

H8096

12

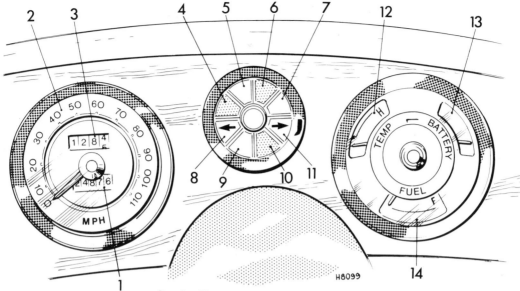

Details of instruments and warning lights

1 Odometer
2 Speedometer
3 Trip odometer
4 Oil pressure warning light
5 High beam warning light
6 Ignition warning light
7 Fuel low level warning
   light
8 Left-hand indicator light
9 Choke warning light
10 Handbrake warning light
11 Right-hand indicator light
12 Temperature gauge
13 Battery indicator
   (ammeter on 1300 models
   models)
14 Fuel gauge

when you first start up because, especially on higher mileage cars, it could take a few seconds for the oil to circulate through the cold engine, and considerable wear can occur to some of the bearings and major moving parts through over-revving.

Choke warning light

The choke warning light illuminates when the choke control knob is pulled out and extinguishes when the knob is pushed fully home. If the light remains on with the choke knob pushed right in and the engine running smoothly, there is probably a fault in the warning light circuit and there is not much to worry about. However, if the engine runs roughly, the choke linkage is probably at fault and this should be checked immediately.

Fuel warning light

The fuel warning light will illuminate when the content of the fuel tank falls below 1.5 gallons (6.8 litres). As the level of fuel drops towards this amount, the light may glow intermittently due to fuel surge.

Handbrake warning light

This light will illuminate when the handbrake is applied with the ignition on and extinguish when the handbrake is fully released. If the light stays on after the handbrake has been fully released there is probably a fault in the light circuit and the car can be driven quite safely although the light circuit should be checked as soon as possible.

Instruments

Temperature gauge

Both the 1300 and 1500 models are fitted with a temperature gauge located on the right-hand side instrument dial and it's a good idea to make a habit of checking it now and again when you're driving, particularly on long journeys. What the gauge tells you is the temperature of the cooling water circulating around the engine, and on the gauge itself there are two sectors, a 'C' and an 'H'. Normally, the needle should remain somewhere around the mid portion of the gauge but, if it happens to be a very hot summer's day the needle may creep up towards the 'H' sector especially if you're trapped in a long line of holiday traffic. Should the needle move into the 'H' sector, you've got to start scratching your head because the engine doesn't take too kindly to **13** overheating. If you're in a queue of traffic, and to stop would be dangerous, try moving the heater control to the hot position and the air distribution control to the interior, floor and windscreen positions; then turn the heater boost fan on full blast. You'll probably need to open all your car windows but at least you're helping to release some of the engine heat, and the temperature gauge may begin to move back to normal. However, if it still remains in the 'H' sector, you should switch off the engine, open the bonnet and investigate the problem. You may have a water leak, or the thermostat may be causing trouble, but your first aim must be to let the engine cool down. Checking your temperature gauge regularly could save you quite a lot of money if you take the right action quickly.

Battery charge indicator or Voltmeter (1500 models)

Both these instruments are in fact voltmeters and as such will indicate the electrical system voltage under varying operating conditions. If you turn the ignition key to position II (that's ignition and accessories 'ON') the gauge needle, after about 45 seconds, will register the static battery voltage and, if all is well, the needle should be at a point in the first sector of the gauge. When the engine's started and running normally the needle should indicate approximately 14 volts and remain there, indicating that the battery and charging system are functioning correctly. Problems occur if the needle stays at a high or low reading for any length of time, which indicates an insufficient or excessive battery charge rate; then you've got a charging fault which should be investigated immediately.

Ammeter

The 1300 models are fitted with an ammeter which indicates the rate the battery is being charged. After initial engine start up the needle should move towards the 'C' mark and then gradually drop back to the centre position after the car has been driven for a few miles. If the needle swings towards the 'D' position the battery is not being charged and the fault should be checked immediately.

Switches (1300 models)

Lighting switches

A master lighting switch is located on the left-hand side of the instrument panel and a lighting selector stalk type switch is on the left-hand side of the steering column. Switching on the master switch and moving the selector stalk upwards will illuminate the sidelights and number plate lights only. Moving the selector stalk downwards to the centre position

illuminates the headlight main beams. Further downward movement of the stalk switches the headlights to the dipped position. Pulling the stalk back towards the steering wheel will flash the headlights without having to switch the master light switch on. A roof light switch and instrument panel illumination control switch are also on the left-hand side of the instrument panel.

Windscreen wiper and washer switches

The wipers are controlled by a simple on/off toggle switch on the right-hand side of the instrument panel. Above the wiper switch is the washer control knob. Pressing the knob in and out will spray water on the windscreen and the wipers should then be switched on until the screen is clear.

Direction indicator switch

This is the control stalk on the right-hand side of the steering column. The stalk is pushed downwards for the right-hand indicators and upwards for the left-hand indicators. Repeater lights are on the central warning panel.

Horn switch

The horns are operated by pressing the bar in the centre of the steering wheel.

Switches (1500 models)

The layout of the switches on the 1500 models differs completely from the 1300 models as they are all operated by means of multi-functional switches attached to the steering column.

Master light switch

This is the rotary switch on the right-hand side of the steering column (D in illustration). Turning the switch clockwise from the OFF position switches on the sidelights and instrument panel lights. A second clockwise movement of the switch illuminated the headlights.

Multi-function switch

This is the control stalk projecting from the right-hand side of the steering column (see illustration) which has the following functions:

Positon A – Pressing the end of the lever operates the horn.

Position B – Providing the master light switch is in the headlight position, pushing the lever forward from the centre (high beam) position will dip the headlight beams.

Position C – Pulling the lever rearwards towards the steering wheel will flash the headlights.

Positions L and R – Pushing the lever upwards operates the left-hand direction indicator lights while

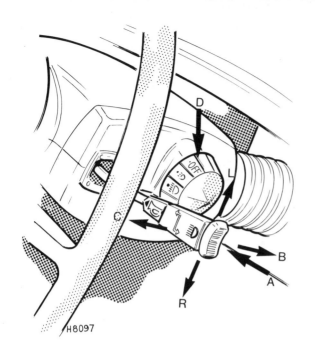

Master light switch and combination switch fitted to 1500 models

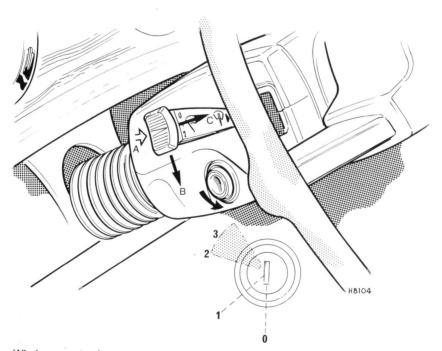

Windscreen wiper/washer and horn switch and details of ignition switch — 1500 models

downward movement of the lever operates the right-hand indicator lights.

Windscreen wiper and washer switch

This is the control stalk projecting from the left-hand side of the steering column, (see illustration). The switch operates as follows:

Position A – Pressing the end of the lever will operate the windscreen washers.

Position B – Moving the lever downwards to the first position switches the windscreen wipers on to the slow speed. A second downward movement of the lever selects a fast wiper speed.

Position C – With the wipers in the OFF position, pulling the lever rearwards towards the steering wheel enables the wipers to be switched on for brief periods if required. When the lever is released the wipers will stop.

Ignition switch/steering column lock

The 1300 models are fitted with a conventional ignition switch (see illustration), but on the 1500 models the ignition switch is also used to actuate a steering column lock. The ignition switch has four positions. In Position 'O' the ignition's switched off and the steering column's locked when the ignition key's removed, although in some circumstances the steering can still be locked with the ignition key inserted. In position 1 the steering's unlocked and the ignition remains off, but accessories such as the radio can be switched on; you may have to move the steering wheel a little when you select this position to release the locking mechanism. In position 2 the ignition's switched on already for starting (one point in passing — don't leave the ignition switch in this position too long with the engine stopped or you may overheat the ignition coil). Position 3 operates the starter, but if the engine fails to start after releasing the key, you'll have to select position 1 again before making another attempt' this prevents the starter operating with the engine running, an action which could damage the starter and flywheel gears.

If you have the misfortune to be towed at any time, the manufacturers recommend that the ignition key is turned to position 2. Although in position 1 the steering's unlocked, this is an extra safety precaution to prevent the car steering you instead of you steering the car, so it's always wise to follow this advice. In these circumstances you'll need to disconnect the battery negative lead and tie it down away from the battery to avoid overheating the ignition coil and circuit.

Steering column adjustment

The steering column can be adjusted both vertically and axially to enable the driver to achieve

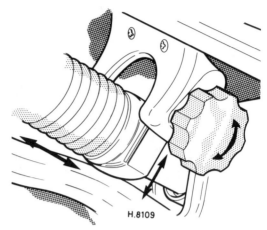

Steering column adjusting knob – 1300 model illustrated

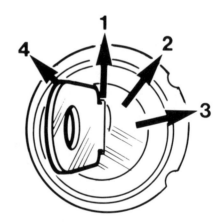

1. OFF
2. IGNITION
3. START
4. AUXILIARY

Ignition switch fitted to 1300 models

the most comfortable driving position. To adjust the column, turn the clamping knob on the right-hand side of the column anti-clockwise. Move the column to the required position and tighten the clamping knob.

Gear selector lever

The floor mounted gear lever selects the four forward gears by moving it in the usual 'H' configuration starting with 1st gear in the forward left position and working up through the gears to 4th

which is in rear right of the 'H'. To select reverse gear, position the gear lever in the neutral position and then push it as far as it will go to the left against the spring resistance and then forwards. Note that reverse gear should only be engaged when the car is stationary as, unlike the forward gears it is not equipped with synchromesh.

Heater controls

The heater controls are simple to use, and the

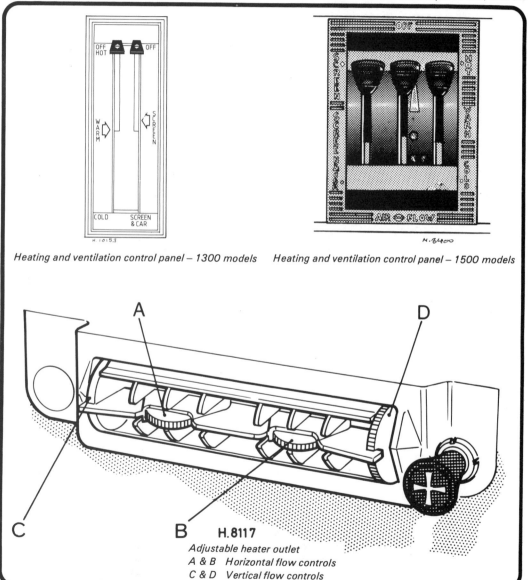

Heating and ventilation control panel – 1300 models   *Heating and ventilation control panel – 1500 models*

H.8117
Adjustable heater outlet
A & B   Horizontal flow controls
C & D   Vertical flow controls

accompanying illustrations are largely self-explanatory. On 1300 models the left-hand lever controls the temperature of the air entering the passenger compartment. Moving the lever down the quadrant progressively increases the volume of cold air in the air mixture and lowers the air temperature. The right-hand lever controls the air distribution. With both levers at the top of the quadrant the system is turned off. During hot weather when cold air circulation is required, it may be necessary to close the water valve control on the dashboard to cut water circulation to the heater unit, otherwise the incoming air may still be slightly warm. A heater blower is incorporated in the system to increase the airflow when required.

The controls for 1500 models differ from 1300 models. In addition to the main heating and ventilation system, there is an 'eyeball' fresh air vent situated at each end of the dash panel. These can be swivelled in their sockets to direct the airflow, and a knob at the centre of each vent can be used to control the volume of airflow or to close the vent completely.

A central panel contains three levers. The left-hand one controls air distribution to the car interior as for the 1300 models. The right-hand one controls the air temperature as for the 1300 models, but in addition closes the water valve control when at its lowest position (the 1300 has a separate water valve control situated on the dashboard). The central lever controls the volume of air passing through the heating/ventilation system. When at its lower (maximum volume) range of travel it operates the blower motor, first at low speed, and upon further downward movement, at higher speed.

An additional variable heater outlet is provided on 1500 models and is shown in the accompanying illustration. The knobs A and B control airflow in a horizontal direction and knobs C and D control airflow in the vertical plane. The airflow can be completely shut off by turning C and D fully in either direction. For maximum airflow to the windscreen for defrosting, this outlet should be closed.

Filling Station Facts

Listed on a following page are those facts and figures that you'll need to know from time to time when visiting the service station. They're designed as a quick reference so that you don't have to ask the petrol pump attendant (who probably won't know anyway) or have to pester the mechanics, who are usually too busy with other matters to bother.

Topping up oil

Whenever you top up the oil level, always try to use the same grade and brand; and do avoid using cheap oil – the initial saving will probably be lost in increased engine wear over a prolonged period – or perhaps a short one!

When checking the oil level, ensure that the car's standing on level ground. Take out the dipstick, wipe it clean, then replace it fully. Pull it out again and note the oil level. Under no circumstances should the level be allowed to drop below the 'MIN' mark. If the oil level is at this mark, about 2 pints (1 litre) will be needed to bring it up to 'MAX'. Avoid over-filling and wipe up any oil spilt.

Checking coolant level

If the engine's at its normal running temperature or higher, **take extra care** when removing the overflow reservoir filler cap. Place a rag over the cap, turn slowly anti-clockwise to the first position, and allow the pressure in the system to escape, then again turn anti-clockwise and remove carefully.

If a considerable amount of water's required to top up or you're continually adding water during the winter months, the antifreeze mixture will be diluted and made less effective. So if antifreeze is in use, topping up should be done with water/antifreeze mixture in the correct proportions.

The coolant level should be brought up to half fill the reservoir. Make sure that the pressure cap's properly fitted afterwards.

Tyre pressures

When checking tyre pressures, don't forget to check the pressure in the spare – in the event of a puncture you could be in for a 'let down'! If you're affluent enough to have your own tyre pressure gauge, always use this to check the pressures – garage gauges aren't always terribly accurate and it's essential that the pressures are right to ensure the correct handling of the car when steering and braking.

Remember that tyre pressures can only be checked accurately when the tyres are cold. Any tyre that's travelled more than a mile or so will show a pressure increase of several pounds per square inch (psi) – maybe more than 5 psi after a longer run. So a certain amount of 'guesstimation' comes into checking tyres if they're warm.

Since the pressures won't have increased for any reason other than heat, the least you can do is to ensure that the pressures in the two front tyres are equal, bearing in mind that they may be a bit above those shown in the table. (The same applies to the two back tyres, but remember that their pressure may be different from the front ones).

If one tyre of a pair has a low pressure when hot, bring it up to the pressure of the other at the same end of the car; if they're both below the recommended cold pressure although warm, the safest thing to do is to bring them up to about 3 psi above it, to allow for cooling.

Self-service garages

Many garages now operate on a self-service basis so that the customer's subjected to the intricacies of refuelling his or her own vehicle. Regulars to this type of establishment need no introduction to its methods of operation and can usually be seen going through the routine at high speed like well-oiled robots. To the newcomer, the operation of the various kinds of pump can at first be confusing, but don't panic! Carefully read each instruction on the pump and in turn before attempting to work it. When refuelling insert the nozzle fully into the car's filler tube and try to regulate the fuel flow at an even rate so that it's not too fast. Most pumps now have an automatic flow-back valve mechanism fitted in them, which prevents any surplus petrol making a speedy exit from the filler neck all over the unsuspecting operator. On completion, don't forget to refit your petrol filler cap!

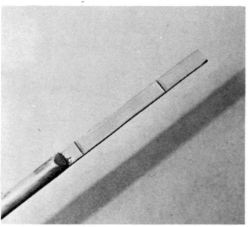

Oil dipstick showing maximum and minimum marks

QUICK-CHECK CHART

TYRE PRESSURES

Recommended pressures in psi (kgf/cm²) for cold tyres

	Front	Rear
1300 models	22 (1.55)	22 (1.55)
1500 models	26 (1.83)	26 (1.83)

Note: rear tyre pressures should be increased by 4 psi (0.28 kgf/cm²) when the car is fully laden

FUEL OCTANE RATING
1300 (except TC) and 1500 models	94 octane (3 star)
1300 TC models	97 octane (4 star)

FUEL TANK CAPACITY
1300 models	11.75 gallons (53.4 litres)
1500 models	12.5 gallons (57 litres)

COOLING SYSTEM CAPACITY
1300 models	6.25 pints (3.5 litres)
1500 models	8.5 pints (4.8 litres)

ENGINE OIL TYPE
All models	20W-50 multigrade

QUANTITY OF OIL REQUIRED TO BRING DIPSTICK LEVEL FROM 'MIN' TO 'MAX' (APPROX)
All models	2 pints (1.14 litres)

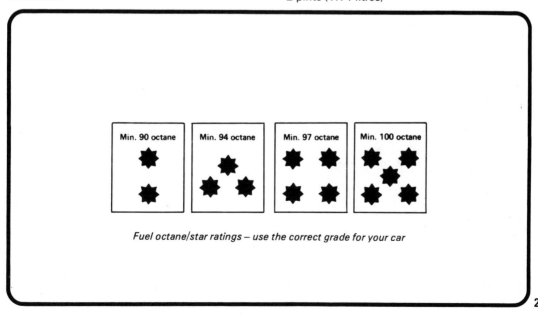

Fuel octane/star ratings – use the correct grade for your car

In an Emergency

There's been no car yet invented that can guarantee you a safe and reliable journey from A to B every day of your life. Be it due to a breakdown or a puncture, the day will come when your trusty transport requires a bit of roadside attention — usually at the most inconvenient time. In this Handbook you'll find a wealth of information which should certainly minimise the possibility of a breakdown but, although we hope it won't be very often, the odd thing's bound to go wrong from time to time.

The Troubleshooter Charts should help to trace the cause of an unexpected problem, but it's not much good knowing what's wrong if you've got nothing to put it right with, or needing to change a wheel in the dark when you haven't a clue how the jack works. A few timely moments spent reading through this Chapter now could save your time and temper later on!

Spares and repairs kit

The basic 'tools' supplied with the car will enable you to change a wheel and that's about the limit. It's pretty obvious that an additional tool kit is required and ought to be carried in the car. For more information on this see *Tools for the Job.*

Along with certain tools it's a good idea to carry a few spare parts and repair items which can be fitted without too much bother at the roadside. These can prove invaluable in getting you out of trouble on the odd occasion when they might be needed. The sort of things you should carry are:

Spark plug, properly cleaned and gapped
HT lead and plug cap — one that will reach the furthest plug from the distributor
Set of light bulbs
Tyre valve core and pocket pressure gauge
Spare fuses
Distributor rotor, condenser and contact set
Fan belt
Roll of insulating tape
Tin of radiator sealer and a hose repair bandage
First aid box and manual
Spare set of keys (but not in the car)
Extension light and lead with crocodile clips
Windscreen de-icer aerosol (during winter months)
Breakdown triangle
Clean lint-free cloth
This Handbook or Haynes Workshop Manual

A box like this is useful for keeping your emergency repair kit together

If you want to carry emergency petrol, use an approved safety can of the type shown here. The detachable spout makes pouring easy, too

An 'Instant Spare' aerosol in use on a flat tyre

This list could of course be expanded indefinitely – for example, you might like to have a set of spare cooling system hoses instead of just a hose bandage. It's up to you to decide what you're likely to be able to use in a roadside situation.

We'll mention here just three other items for emergency use which it might make you feel happier to have on board. The first is a 'universal' temporary fan belt which can be fitted without loosening any bolts, and which will enable you to get going again quickly in the event of a belt breakage and to fit a proper replacement belt at your leisure.

The second 'get-you-home' device is an 'instant' puncture repair in the form of an aerosol can. The nozzle is screwed on to the tyre valve, and releases sealant to seal the leak, together with gas to reinflate the tyre. It's suitable for tubed or tubeless tyres, and will at the very least allow you to drive to a garage without getting your hands dirty.

Our third additional suggestion is a temporary windscreen. If you've ever suffered a shattered screen, you'll know what a nightmare it can be trying to drive the car, especially in bad weather. If you haven't, take our word for it! One of the roll-up type of polyester temporary screens is quick and easy to fit, leaves driving unaffected, and wipers and washers can be used normally. When not in use its thin container stows neatly in a corner of the boot or on the back shelf.

It's not normally necessary to carry spare fuel in this country, but if you want to have an extra gallon or so on board for emergencies, do use one of the special safety cans now available. They're not only purpose-built to reduce the risk of fire in an accident, they're so much easier to pour from than a makeshift container.

Jacking up and changing a wheel

All models are equipped with a screw scissor-type jack which engages with square brackets in the underside of the body sill (refer to the illustrations for details). The jack, jack handle, wheelbrace and hub cap removing tool are located in the luggage compartment adjacent to the spare wheel. The spare wheel fits in a well below the floor and is retained by a strap.

To begin the wheel changing operation, first apply the handbrake firmly and engage first or reverse gear then find something to chock the wheels on the other side of the car. An old brick or block of wood is just the job, but unless you carry such a thing you may have to improvise. If you can only find one, weigh up which way the car's likely to move if anything goes wrong, hopefully you'll find two, then one can be put each side of a wheel.

Before lifting, but with the jack correctly **23**

An emergency windscreen is fitted in seconds and can save untold discomfort

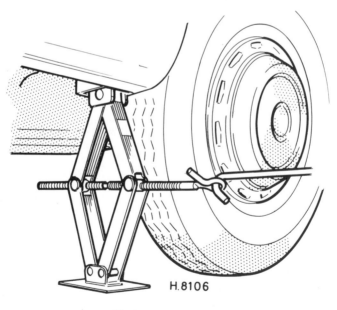

H.8106

Placing the jack in position

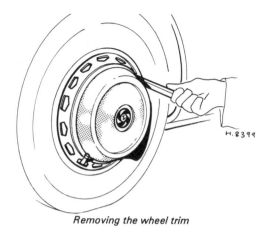

Removing the wheel trim

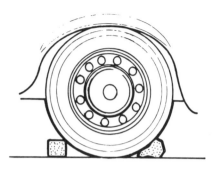

Always wedge the wheels before jacking

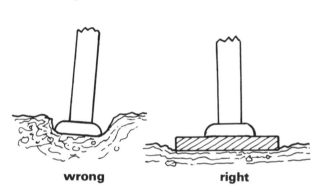

wrong **right**

Spread the load under the foot of the jack

positioned, remove the wheel trim with the tool provided. If you haven't got the angled tool you can use a large screwdriver to lever off the hub cap. Now use the wheel nut spanner to loosen each nut by about half a turn. Hopefully, the nuts won't be too tight but if they are you can apply a bit of foot power on the spanner to loosen them.

The car now be jacked up, but make sure it doesn't move, and check that the chocks are still in position. Take off the wheel nuts and then the wheel. Fit the spare wheel to the car, tighten the wheel nuts up evenly in a diagonal sequence, but do not try to tighten them fully at this stage. Lower the car to the ground and tighten the wheel nuts fully before removing the jack. Before lifting, but with the jack correctly positioned, remove the wheel trim with the tool provided. If you haven't got the angled tool you can use a large screwdriver to lever off the hub cap. Now use the wheel nut spanner to loosen each nut by about half a turn. Hopefully, the nuts won't be too

tight but if they are you can apply a bit of foot power on the spanner to loosen them.

The car can now be jacked up, but make sure it doesn't move, and check that the chocks are still in position. Take off the wheel nuts and then the wheel. Fit the spare wheel to the car, tighten the wheel nuts up evenly in a diagonal sequence, but do not try to tighten them fully at this stage. Lower the car to the ground and tighten the wheel nuts fully before removing the jack.

Towing and being towed

Some models may be fitted with towing eyes located beneath the front and rear bumpers and these can be used for towing or being towed. If your car is not equipped with towing eyes, the towrope or chain should be attached to the rigid suspension crossmembers at the front and rear of the car. During towing you'll have to make adjustments to your driving technique because of the restricted distance **25** between the two vehicles, and don't forget to warn other road users by fixing a suitable notice on the rear of the vehicle being towed.

The most important thing is to use a suitable rope or chain. It must be strong enough for the job, and long enough to allow a safe distance between the vehicles. The maximum distance allowed is 15 feet and whilst no minimum distance is specified, don't have the rope too short or the driver of the towed vehicle could end up with a nervous breakdown as well!

Try to keep the rope taut and prevent if from 'snatching'. This can be achieved by the towing driver making smooth use of the throttle and gearbox. The driver of the towed vehicle can assist by carefully applying the brakes when going downhill and when stopping or slowing.

Maintenance of lights

Since it's an offence to operate a vehicle on the road at any time of the day with any of the full complement of external lights not in working order, it will be useful to at least know how to change a bulb when this becomes necessary. For this reason also, it is a good idea to carry an assortment of replacement bulbs in the car.

The 1300 models have single headlamps while the 1500 models are fitted with dual headlamps. Also depending on the year of manufacture, either sealed beam or bulb type headlamps may be fitted; in all cases the method of removal and refitting is similar and providing reference is made to the relevant illustrations no problems should be encountered.

Headlamp sealed beam or bulb renewal
1300 models

Remove the screw located at the bottom of the rim, and with a wide blade screwdriver carefully prise away the rim from the wing. Undo and remove the three screws which hold the inner rim to the seating rim and lift away the inner rim.

Carefully draw the sealed beam unit forwards until the connector is exposed, and disconnect the sealed beam unit from the connector.

Refitting is a straightforward reversal of the above procedure.

1500 models

Undo and remove the two screws securing the bezel panel and lift away the bezel. Slacken the three screws securing the retaining rim and rotate in an anti-clockwise direction to release the retaining rim and light unit.

If a bulb is fitted, pull the connector from the bulb. Disengage the clip and withdraw the old bulb. Fit a new bulb making sure it is correctly located in the holder.

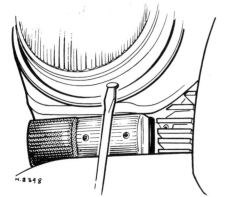

Removing the headlamp rim retaining screw (1300)

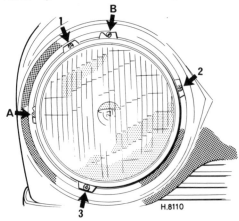

Headlamp sealed beam unit fitted to 1300 models
1, 2 & 3   Retaining screws
A & B   Adjustment screws

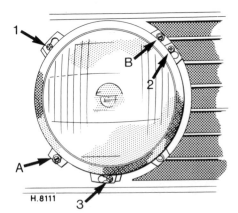

Headlamp units fitted to 1500 models
1, 2 & 3   Retaining screws
A & B   Adjustment screws

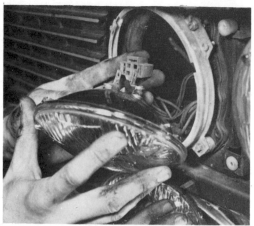

Removing sealed beam unit (1500 models)

Removing front sidelight/flasher light lens (1500 models)

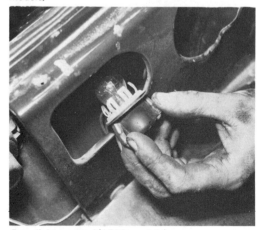

Rear light removal (1500 models)

Where a sealed beam light is fitted, pull the connector from the light unit. Fit a new light unit.

Refitting. is a straightforward reversal of the above procedure.

Headlight alignment

After renewing or disturbing a headlight unit it is advisable to have the headlamps aligned on proper optical equipment, but if this is not available the following procedure should be used.

Position the car on level ground 10 feet (3 metres) in front of a dark wall or board. The wall or board must be at right angles to the centre line of the car, which is marked on the wall or board as a vertical line.

Bounce the car on its suspension to ensure correct settlement and then measure the height between the ground and the centre of the headlamps.

Draw a horizontal line across the board at this measured height and on this line mark off half the distance between the centres of the two headlights starting from the previously marked vertical line. This will give the centres of the headlights.

Remove the headlight rim (1300) or bezel (1500) and switch the headlamps onto full beam.

By carefully adjusting the horizontal and vertical adjusting screws on each lamp, align the centres of each beam onto the marks which were previously made on the horizontal line.

Bounce the car again and check that the beams return to the correct positions. At the same time check the operation of the dip switch. Refit the rim or bezel.

Side and front flasher bulb renewal
1300 models

Unscrew and remove the three crosshead screws securing the two lenses. Lift away the lenses. The relevant bulb is removed from its holder by slightly depressing it and rotating it in an anti-clockwise direction. Refitting is the reverse procedure to removal.

1500 models

Undo and remove the two screws securing the complete light unit to the body. Draw the light unit forwards and remove the old bulb. Fit a new bulb and refit the light unit.

Rear flasher, tail/stop and reverse light bulb renewal
1300 models

Undo and remove the screws that secure the front edge of the boot interior trim. Carefully pull back the trim and remove the applicable bulb holder from the rear of the light unit. Fit a new bulb and refit the **27**

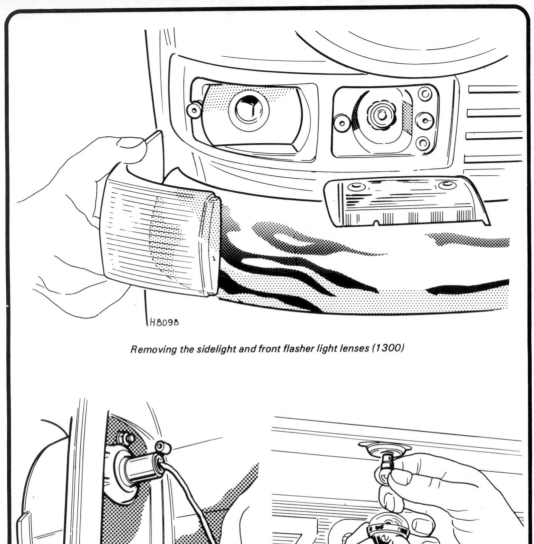

H8098

Removing the sidelight and front flasher light lenses (1300)

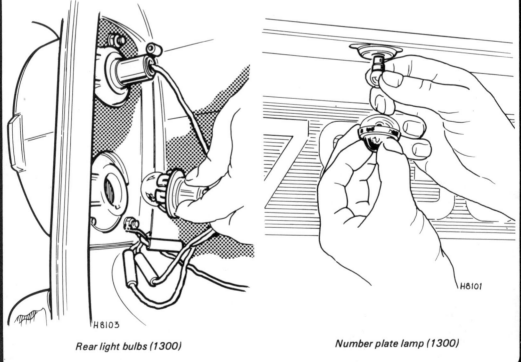

H8103

Rear light bulbs (1300)

H8101

Number plate lamp (1300)

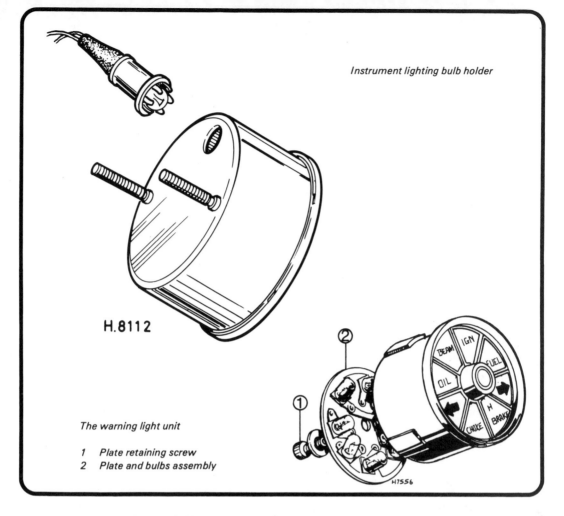

Instrument lighting bulb holder

H.8112

The warning light unit

1   Plate retaining screw
2   Plate and bulbs assembly

H7556

Rear number plate light lens removal (1500 models)

Location of fuses on bulkhead

holder. Refit the interior trim and secure with the screws.

1500 models

Pull up the four fasteners and move the floor matting forwards. Undo and remove the five screws and turn back the rear trim the interior trim and floor matting. Note that a reversing light is also included in the rear light unit. Refitting is a reversal of the removal procedure.

Rear number plate lamp renewal

To renew the bulb undo and remove the two screws and lift off the chrome cover. Disengage the small lugs of the appropriate lens from the rubber base. Remove the bulb and fit a new one. Refit the lens and chrome cover.

Interior roof lamp renewal

Carefully rotate the light lens until the two retaining screws are exposed and undo the screws. Remove the lens and replace the festoon type bulb with a new one. Refit the lens and secure it with the two retaining screws.

Luggage compartment light renewal

Renewal of the luggage compartment light is simply a matter of unscrewing the old bulb from the holder and screwing in a new one.

Panel and warning light bulb renewal

Note: In all cases while you're working behind the instrument panel, detach the battery earth lead for safety's sake.

On 1300 models it is first necessary to remove the choke control knob by pushing in the small plunger on the side of the knob and then pulling off the knob. Also unscrew the choke control bezel from the panel. On all models, adjust the steering column to its lowest rearward position to improve access. Remove the instrument panel retaining screws and withdraw the panel rearwards taking care not to strain the electrical cables. If necessary disconnect the speedometer cable. The panel illumination bulbs can be renewed by pulling the holders from the rear of the instrument casing and unscrewing the bulbs.

In the case of the warning light bulbs it is first necessary to carefully pull off the multi-pin plug from the rear of the warning light cluster and remove the centre retaining screw. Withdraw the bulb holder plate and renew any of the bulbs that have failed.

Refit the instrument panel assembly using the reverse of the removal procedure.

Fuses

The electrical circuits on both the 1300 and 1500 models are protected by two fuses located on the rear engine compartment bulkhead. The following circuits are protected by each fuse:

1300 models

Fuse No 1   Horns and interior light circuits
Fuse No 2   Voltage stabilizer feeding fuel and
                temperature gauge circuits
                Wiper and heater motor circuits
                Flasher unit and associated circuits
                11 RA relay contacts and stop lights

1500 Models

Battery (brown cable) fuse
    Horn
    Headlight flasher
    Cigar lighter
    Luggage boot
    Roof light
Ignition switch (white cable) fuse
    Fuel gauge
    Temperature gauge
    Windscreen wiper
    Stop light
    Heater
    Windscreen washer
    Reversing lamp
    Turn signal indicators

The fuses on all models are 35 amps and if a fuse blows it must be replaced with a fuse of the same rating. If a fuse blows persistently, never try to cure the problem by fitting a fuse with a higher rating; a burnt out wiring harness or worse could result. Instead, inspect the circuits and electrical units which are protected by the fuse for faults.

Changing a broken fan belt

A broken fan belt is sometimes not noticed until the engine's boiling, and if this happens the coolant level should be checked and probably replenished as well as fitting a new fan belt; take special precautions before removing the radiator filler cap (see *Filling Station Facts*).

Refer to *Service Scene* to fit the new belt.

Save It!

For the owner-driver, motoring never has been and probably never will be a cheap pastime. If a car isn't used much, then the running costs may be low, but the few miles travelled in it are comparatively expensive when the initial cost plus subsequent depreciation are taken into account. But obviously the more you use your car, then the maintenance and running costs must correspondingly increase. So you can't win — or can you? Since money is fairly close to most people's hearts, any chance of reducing the annual motoring bill are not to be sniffed at — but how *can* we reduce costs? Let's talk about some of the most important items to be considered from the economic point of view.

Maintenance

To start with, the car must be kept in a good state of tune in order to give the maximum performance combined with reliability. Although a car may start without too much bother each day and transport you from A to B without giving trouble, it may well be operating quite inefficiently and therefore indirectly adding to your costs.

The various components on a car that need regular servicing will continue to function without complaint when neglected, but the working life of these components is invariably shortened so they'll need renewal before it should be necessary.

If you normally take your car to a garage for servicing then you'll no doubt have noticed the ever increasing costs of the labour charges. Unless you can be sure that the garage people you deal with are honourable types, how do you know if the work listed as completed has been carried out properly, if at all?

One of the aims of this book is to encourage owners to do their own servicing which, though you may never have handled even a spanner, is well within the capabilities of the average person. The ironmongery lying beneath your car's bodywork is not nearly so technical and formidable as it may appear.

With a small initial outlay in costs for some basic tools you could, over a period of time, save yourself a considerable sum of money and be a more complete motorist, simply by doing your own basic service tasks. You'll also be able to shop around for the parts required and probably obtain them at cheaper prices than those charged by your garage.

Tyres

Without any doubt whatever, a radial tyre will give you much better value for money than a crossply because, although it will cost a bit more to buy, it will last a great deal longer. Remould tyres can give good service, but they have their limitations when used for family motoring; remould radials now have a more reliable reputation then they had when they first appeared on the market, but sometimes give a bit of trouble when trying to balance them.

So, what have we learnt so far? Only that in the broadest terms the more you pay for your tyres, the better value for money you'll get. If you want the best in roadholding and tyre life, buy radials; if you want reasonable tyre life, but aren't quite so worried about the roadholding under adverse conditions, buy crossplies; if you want a good runabout tyre, and aren't thinking of high speeds or long journeys, buy radial remoulds but remember they may give a bit of steering wheel 'shimmy' if used on the front; if you want the cheapest tyre which still complies with the law in safety standards, buy remould crossplies.

Regraded tyres are sometimes available (they used to be known as remould quality or RQ); these are tyres which may have the very slightest of defects **31**

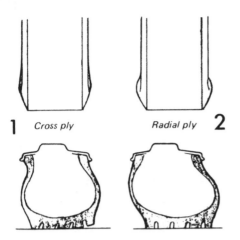

1 Cross ply   Radial ply 2

Cross-ply and radial ply tyres
The difference in the construction of the two types of tyre gives them very different characteristics. The cross-ply (1) has a uniformly strong tread and wall bracing. This gives it better cushioning properties but allows some deformation on bad surfaces and cambers. The radial ply tyre (2) has a supple wall and a firmly braced tread, ensuring that the maximum area of tread is kept in contact with the road despite suspension angle changes and road camber effects. On no account should the two types of tyre be mixed on the same axle. (See the Weekly checks listed in Service Scene*).*

in the tread pattern or moulding, but are otherwise perfect. If you get the chance to buy them, buy them — to all intents and purposes they're as good as a new tyre.

It's not generally realised that the major tyre manufacturers also produce tyres under a less well known name at a somewhat cheaper price. These are first class buys too — ask any tyre dealer.

Talking of tyre dealers, it's worth mentioning that they're the people to go to if you're intent on saving money (and who isn't these days?). Unless there's a 'special offer' going, the most expensive place to get new tyres will normally be your local garage.

Now let's just briefly consider how to make your tyres last. First, keep them inflated properly (see *Filling Station Facts* for the correct pressures). Second, drive in the way that's least likely to wear them out (ie no race-track starts or cornering); third, make sure your shock absorbers are working propely; and fourth, make sure the wheels are balanced properly.

Batteries

Next to tyres, batteries are the most commonly found parts sold by specialists. A top quality battery may cost up to three times the price of the cheapest one that'll fit your car.

Once again, price is related to the quality of the product, but isn't necessarily directly proportioned. A battery with a twelve month guarantee ought to last that long and little bit more, but batteries always seem to fail at embarrassing or inconvenient times so it's worthwhile getting something a little bit better. Many of the accessory shops and tyre dealers sell good quality batteries with two or three year

guarantees. Buy one of these — it'll be worthwhile in the long run and still cost quite a bit less than the dearest ones around. And if you look after it, it'll look after you, too.

Exhaust systems

The average car gets through several exhaust systems in the course of its life, the actual number depending on the sort of journeys for which the car's used (lots of short journeys will mean condensation remaining inside the exhaust system and helping it to rust out more quickly).

The best place to go when your car needs a replacement exhaust (or maybe just part of the system) is one of the specialist 'exhaust centres' which have sprung up in recent years. They keep huge stocks to fit most mass-produced cars, and offer free fitting as well as discount prices on the parts themselves. You'll almost certainly show a worthwhile saving compared with getting your BL Cars dealer to fit the exhaust (which will involve labour charges as well).

If you're planning to keep your car for several years it would certainly be worth thinking about an exhaust system made from stainless steel. It'll normally cost you considerably more than an ordinary mild steel replacement, but on the other hand should last the remainder of the car's life. If you're interested talk it over with one of the exhaust specialists — they're usually stockists of the stainless steel kind too.

Lubricants and the like

Good cheap engine oils are available, but because it's so difficult to find out which cheap ones *are* good, it's safest to stay clear of them. There are plenty of good multigrade engine oils on the market and quite a few are available at sensible prices from D-I-Y motoring and accessory shops.

Unless circumstances should force you to, don't buy oil in pint or half-litre cans. This is the most expensive way of buying, particularly if it's from a filling station. The big 5-litre (they used to be one gallon) cans are adequate for most purposes and contain more than enough for an oil change. If your pride and joy's a bit of an oil burner, you may need an extra can for topping up between oil changes.

Oil is also available in larger drums (which can be fitted with a tap) sometimes at an even bigger price saving. A telephone call or visit to nearby wholesalers may well prove worthwhile.

Antifreeze is always cheaper if you go to the motoring shops, but bulk buying doesn't normally apply because you never need to buy it in any real quantity.

As for greases, brake fluid, etc, you'll save a little at the motoring shops but again you'll never need large quantities — just make sure that you buy something that's good quality.

Fuel

Your car's designed to run on a particular grade of fuel (star rating). Don't buy fuel that's of a higher rating than this, because you're wasting your money. On the other hand, if you buy a lower rating fuel your engine performance (and probably your engine too) will suffer. If you *are* forced to buy inferior fuel, drive carefully until you can get the correct grade; in these circumstances it's also beneficial to retard the ignition by a couple of degrees, but you've got the bother of resetting it again later.

Smiths Industries 'Milemiser', a type of engine performance or vacuum gauge, can significantly improve fuel economy by monitoring driving technique

Additives

Oil and fuel additives have been with us for a long time and no doubt will be around for many years to come. It's pretty unlikely that there are any bad additives around, but there's not a great deal of evidence to suggest that there are many good ones. The major oil manufacturers will tell you that their oils are adequate on their own, in which case you'll only need additives if the oil you're using isn't much good. A fuel additive of the upper cylinder lubricant type is generally accepted as a good thing, one of its main functions being to prevent carbon building up around the piston rings and ring grooves, which means that the piston rings can seal more effectively.

Economy devices

If we could believe everything published about economy devices, we'd be able to fit the lot and end up with a car that would save more fuel than it used! Obviously this isn't going to happen, and the evidence produced by the motoring magazine doesn't lend much weight to the various manufacturers arguments. If you're considering fitting any of these items (which range from manifold modifiers to spark boosters and fuel pressure regulators), try to get hold of some independent reports before parting with your money.

Vacuum gauge

Also known as a performance gauge or fuel consumption gauge, this can loosely be termed an economy device because its purpose is to tell you how to use performance in the most efficient way. An engine that's running efficiently will be using all the fuel/air mixture in the inlet manifold for any given throttle opening, and in doing so it causes a fairly high suction past the throttle butterfly. The maximum suction it can produce varies, but could be over 20 inches of mercury (that's around 10 psi) relative to atmospheric pressure. If you've got one of these gauges, (and there's some information about fitting one in *the Personal Touch*) try to drive with the maximum vacuum reading all the time and you'll certainly save some money on fuel.

Engine tuning

To the average motorist, this term means getting the best in the way of performance and economy from the car, but some may prefer an increase in performance to such an extent that economy will have to suffer, or vice versa. One thing's sure, unless you're a specialist you won't be able to improve on the specifications and settings laid down by the car manufacturer for your particular model, so these must be your obvious guidelines. You may be able to get different needles for the carburettors, but the power **33** output will probably be affected.

By far the most important factor is to keep your engine regularly maintained, and this means periodically checking the spark plugs, distributor points, ignition timing, carburettor adjustments and valve clearances as detailed later in this Handbook. If you do this, your engine will provide you with the best performance and economy possible.

Driving habits

With the car in a decent state of tune, there's a lot that you, yourself, can do to improve the car's economy simply by your method of driving. It's very tempting at times to do a 'grand prix' start from the traffic lights, or to change down and floor the accelerator just to show yourself that you can do it (nobody else cares anyway!).

The art of economical driving is to use the pedals sensibly. There's no need to race the engine and let the clutch slip violently when starting off; a moderate engine speed, and careful engagement of the clutch, will produce the same result with much greater economy, and only a little more slowly. Once moving, try keeping the throttle pedal in the same position while the car accelerates – you may need to ease it down just a little more, but don't press it too hard – there's just no need for it. The little time saved in accelerating will be outweighed by the additional time and cost involved the next time you fill up with petrol.

Changing through the gears should be done in just the same way, using the accelerator pedal with care. When you have to change down, there's no need to rev your engine – this is another fuel waster. Similarly, 'blipping' the throttle pedal while impatiently waiting for the lights to turn green is using unnecessary fuel.

Even in warm weather you'll need to use the choke to start a cold engine. The secret, though (unless your car has an automatic choke) is to push in the knob as soon as possible; experiment to see how soon it can be done – you may surprise yourself. Excessive use of the choke not only affects fuel economy, but results in unburnt mixture getting into the oil and excessive engine wear. Considerably more engine wear occurs in a few hundred miles of stop/start motoring from cold, than in many times this mileage of driving with a thoroughly warmed-up engine on long journeys.

Roof racks

The ever-faithful roof rack has proved a boon to so many motorists for the extra holiday luggage, but how often do you see cars being driven around with an empty roof rack still attached? Many estimates have been made of the increase in fuel consumption caused by a roof rack due to wind resistance, and the generally accepted figure is around 10%; with a loaded rack, this figure can be as high as 30%. The moral, then, is obvious – don't use a roof rack unless you have to, and always remove it when it's not in use.

Insurance

Like some of the other things that we've discussed, the service you're going to get from your insurance company will be related to the cost of the cover obtained. A cheap policy's good until you need to make a claim, and then the sort of snags you're going to come across are 'How do I get hold of an assessor to inspect the damage?' or 'How will it affect my No Claims Bonus?'

There are one or two legitimate ways of reducing the policy premium, perhaps by insuring for 'owner driver only', or 'two named drivers', or an agreement to pay the first £20 or so of any claim. Many large companies have a discount scheme for their employees if they use the same insurance company; this also applies to bank and Civil Service employees. You may also get a better bargain by insuring through one of the Motoring Associations if you're a member.

What it all adds up to is : (1) insure well; (2) See what you can get in the way of discounts; and (3) Find out exactly what you're covered for.

Buying spare parts

Apart from the oils and greases which you're going to need, it won't be long before you have to buy a few bits and pieces to keep things running smoothly. Please do remember to clean up any parts which are traded-in on an exchange basis (eg brake shoes) and, whenever possible, check that any replacement parts look the same as the old ones, either by direct comparison if this can be done, or by reference to any of the illustrations in the appropriate Section of this book.

Spare parts and accessories are available from many sources, but the following should act as a good guide when they're required.

Officially appointed BL Cars garages: Although a BL Cars garage should be able to supply just about everything for your car, it will generally be found that the prices are higher than you need pay.

Other garages: In recent years the big British car manufacturers have introduced a replacement parts scheme whereby they market parts for each other's cars under trade names such as Mopar, Unipart and Motorcraft. You'll pay the same prices as you would from the BL Cars dealer, but you may well find that your local Chrysler or Ford dealer can supply you with guaranteed parts for your Triumph, and that can't be a bad thing.

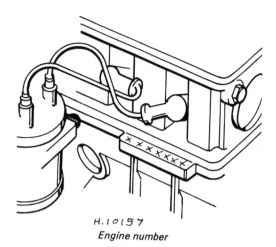

H. 10155

Vehicle identification plate

H. 10157

Engine number

Accessory shops: These are usually the best places for getting your distributor contact breaker points, oil filters, brakes shoes, spark plugs, fan belts, lubricants, touch-up paints etc – the very things you're going to need for the general servicing of the car. They also sell general accessories and charge lower prices but, what's equally important, they have convenient opening hours and can often be found not too far from home.

Motor factors: Good factors will stock all the more important components of the engine, gearbox, suspension and braking systems, and often provide guaranteed parts on an exchange basis. They're particularly useful to the more advanced do-it-yourself motorist.

Vehicle identification numbers

When you're buying spares, the storeman will need to know certain information about your car. The very least he'll need to know is the make, model,engine size and year of manufacture. For some parts he'll have to be told the car's engine number, the vehicle serial number and the service code (which you always meant to take a note of but never got round to doing it!). Make a note of these now in your diary or perhaps the inside cover of this Handbook.

The chassis or commission number is stamped on a plate attached to the inner side of the left-hand wing panel. The engine number is stamped on a flat surface of the cylinder block immediately below the number 4 (rear) spark plug.

Vital Statistics

The specifications given below include all the details you're likely to require during routine service tasks. Certain items such as tyre pressures and fuel tank capacity are given in *Filling Station Facts.* This section may not make very interesting bedtime reading, but it's an indispensable form of reference for Triumph owners.

ENGINE

Type	4 cylinder in-line pushrod operated (ohv)
Bore	73·7 mm (2·9 in)
Stroke	
1300	76 mm (2·99 in)
1500	87·5 mm (3·44 in)
Cubic capacity	
1300	1246 cc (79·2 cu in)
1500	1493 cc (91 cu in)
Compression ratio	
1300 (except TC) and 1500	8·5 : 1
1300 TC	9 : 1
Maximum bhp	
1300 (except TC)	61 at 5000 rpm
1300 TC	75 at 6000 rpm
1500	61 at 5000 rpm
Maximum torque	
1300 (except TC)	73 lbf ft (10·1 kgf m) at 3000 rpm
1300 TC	75 lbf ft (10·2 kgf m) at 4000 rpm
1500	81 lbf ft (11·2 kgf m) at 2700 rpm
Firing order	1 – 3 – 4 – 2
Valve clearances (cold)	0·010 in (0·25 mm)
Sump capacity with filter	6·5 pints (3·5 litres)

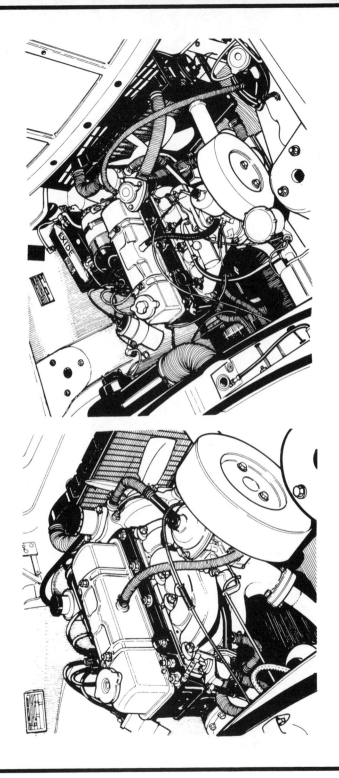

Underbonnet views – 1300 (left), 1500 (right)

COOLING SYSTEM
Type   Pressurised radiator, thermo-syphon, pump assisted and fan cooled

Coolant capacity (with heater)
1300   6·25 pints (3·5 litres)
1500   8·5 pints (4·84 litres)

Blow-off pressure of radiator cap
1300 prior to commission No. RD59522   7 lbf/in² (0·49 kgf/cm²)
1300 and 1500 after commission No. RD 59522   13 lbf/in² (0·91 kgf/cm²)
Fan   4 blades, 12·5 in (31·65 cm) diameter

FUEL SYSTEM
Tank capacity
1300   11·75 gallons (53·4 litres)
1500   12·5 gallons (57 litres)

Carburettors
1300 (except TC)   Zenith Stromberg 150 CD
1300 TC   SU HS2 (twin)
1500   SU HS2

Fuel pump   AC mechanical, driven from camshaft

IGNITION SYSTEM
Distributor type   Lucas 25D4

Contact points gap   0·015 in (0·381 mm)

Static ignition timing
Single carburettor   9° BTDC
Twin carburettor   6° BTDC

Spark plugs   Champion N-9Y or AC Delco 41-4XLS (14 mm)

Plug gap   0·025 in (0·64 mm)

CLUTCH
Type   Single dry plate diaphragm spring

Actuation   Hydraulic

Diameter
1300   6·5 in (165 mm) diameter
1500   7·35 in (184 mm) diameter

GEARBOX
Lubricant capacity   2·25 pints (1·3 litres)

Ratios	*1300*	*1500*
First	3·40	3·02
Second	2·16	1·918
Third	1·45	1·289
Top	1·06	0·889
Reverse	3·99	3·60

38 *Overall gear ratios can be calculated as equal to gearbox ratios x final drive ratio*

Cutaway view of Triumph 1300

Hatton

FINAL DRIVE

Location   Integral unit with gearbox and engine; hypoid bevel gears

Oil capacity   1·25 pints (0·85 litre)

Ratios
1300	4·11 : 1
1500	4·55 : 1

STEERING

Type   Alford and Adler rack and pinion

Turning circle   33 ft (10·06 m) approx

Steering rack oil capacity   0·25 pint (0·15 litre)

SUSPENSION

Front   Independent, double wishbones and coil springs

Rear
1300	Independent, semi-trailing arms, and coil springs
1500	Beam axle, non-independent, trailing link and coil springs

Shock absorbers   Telescopic, hydraulic

WHEELS AND TYRES

Wheels   Steel disc type, 4 stud fitting

Rim size   13 in (330 mm) 4S section

Type
1300	Dunlop C41
1500	Dunlop D75

Pressures (cold)
Front – 1300	22 lbf/in^2 (1·55 kgf/cm^2)
Front – 1500	26 lbf/in^2 (1·83 kgf/cm^2)
Rear – 1300	22 lbf/in^2 (1·55 kgf/cm^2)*
Rear – 1500	26 lbf/in^2 (1·83 kgf/cm^2)

*Rear pressure may be decreased by 4 lbf/in^2 (0·28 kgf/cm^2) in the one- and two-up condition to provide optimum ride.

BRAKES

Type   Girling hydraulic, disc at front, drum at rear

Footbrake   Hydraulic on all four wheels

Handbrake   Mechanical to rear wheels only

Front brakes disc diameter   8·75 in (222 mm)

Rear brakes size
1300	8 x 1·25 in (203·2 x 3·175 mm)
40 1500	8 x 1·5 in (203·2 x 3·81 mm)

Disc brake details

Minimum pad lining thickness	0·125 in (3·18 mm)
Maximum disc run-out	0·002 to 0·004 in (0·0508 to 0·1016 mm)
Disc pad material	Don 212
Front pad lining area	14·8 sq in (955 sq cm)
Front swept area:	
1300	145 sq in (9350 sq cm)
1500	165 sq in (10650 sq cm)

Drum brake details:

Rear lining area	38 sq in (2450 sq cm)
Shoe lining material	Don 24
Minimum lining thickness	0·0625 in (1·588 mm)
Rear swept area:	
1300	63 sq in (4060 sq cm)
1500	75·5 sq in (4870 sq cm)
Adjustment:	
1300	Manually operated adjuster
1500	Self-adjusting mechanism

ELECTRICAL SYSTEM

Battery	12 volt lead acid
Earthed terminal	Negative (–)
Dynamo (1300)	Lucas C40–1
Alternator (1500)	Lucas 15 ACR
Control box (1300)	Lucas RB 340
Fuses	2 mounted on bulkhead

BULBS

1300 models	*Wattage*
Headlamps (sealed beam)	60/45
Side parking	6
Front direction indicator	21
Rear direction indicator	21
Stop	6/21
Warning light cluster	1·5
Roof lamp	6
Number plate light	5
Instrument illumination	2·2

1500 models	
Front parking	5
Front flasher	21
Rear flasher	21
Tail/stop	5/21
Reverse	21
Number plate light	5
Luggage boot illumination	2·2
Roof lamp	6
Instrument illumination	2·2

Warning light cluster	1·5	
Cigarette lighter illumination	2·2	

Dimensions
Wheelbase	8 ft 0·6 in (245·4 cm)
Length – 1300	12 ft 11 in (393·7 cm)
Length – 1500	13 ft 6 in (411 cm)
Width	5 ft 1·75 in (156·8 cm)
Height	4 ft 6 in (132·7 cm)
Ground clearance	5·5 in (14 cm)

Weights
	1300	*1500*
Dry	17 cwt (843 kg)	18 cwt (915 kg)
Kerb	18 cwt (914 kg)	19 cwt (965 kg)
Max gross vehicle weight	23·25 cwt (118 kg)	26 cwt (1315 kg)

Tools for the Job

For anyone intending to tackle car servicing, a selection of good down-to-earth tools is a basic requirement. The initial outlay, even though it may appear to be something approaching the national defence budget, could well be less than the labour charges for one full service; on top of this, you should be paying less for the oil and replacement parts by getting them yourself, so provided you've two or three hours to spare, you must be on to a winner.

The 'tools' supplied with the car will enable you to jack it up and change a wheel, and that's all. So if you're serious about doing your own servicing, a basic additional tool kit is absolutely essential.

A small but important point when buying tools is the quality. You don't have to buy the very best in the shop but, on the other hand, the cheapest probably aren't much good. Have a word with the manager or proprietor if you're in doubt. He'll tell you what's good value for money.

It's very difficult to tell you exactly what you're going to need, but the list below should be a great help in building up a good tool kit. Combination spanners (ring one-end, open-ended the other) are recommended because, although more expensive than double open-ended ones, they give the advantages of both types.

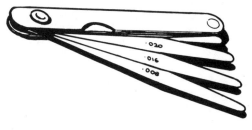

Feeler gauges

Combination spanners to cover the range $\frac{1}{4}$ to 1 in AF
Adjustable spanner – 9 inch
Spark plug spanner (with rubber insert)
Spark plug gap adjustment tool
Set of feeler gauges
Brake adjuster spanner ($\frac{1}{4}$in AF, square)
Screwdriver – 4 in blade x $\frac{1}{4}$ in dia (flat blade)
Screwdriver – 4 in blade x $\frac{1}{4}$ dia (cross blade)
Pliers – 6 inch
Junior hacksaw
Tyre pump
Tyre pressure gauge
Grease gun

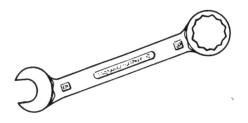

Combination ring/open-ended spanner

43

Oil can
Fine emery cloth or oilstone
Wire brush (small)
Funnel (medium size)
Hydraulic jack or strong scissor type
Pair of axle stands (concrete or wooden blocks
will do if you're careful about choosing them)
Hose brush

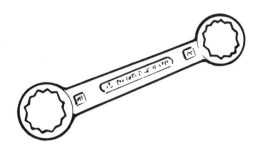

Double ended ring spanner

You may find that a pair of metal ramps is a very useful investment, providing an alternative to the jack or axle stands when you want to get at the underside of the car but don't need to remove the wheel(s). Most ramps available give a lift of between 9 inches and 1 ft and you can, of course, drive either the front or back end of the car on to them – but you'll still need to engage a gear and chock the other two wheels for safety's safe.

Hopefully, your attempts at car servicing are going to show you that it can all be worthwhile, and having worked your way through the various jobs listed in *Service Scene* you'll be able to see that there are many others which can be done without becoming a mechanical wizard. For this purpose, Haynes publish a first class Owner's Workshop Manual for the Triumph 1300/1500 which details just about every operation that can conceivably be done on these cars. It'll mean buying a few more tools, but to hell with it – you're out to save yourself some money and get a good job done in the process.

While we're talking about tools, it's worth mentioning some of the tune-up aids that are on the market. A visit to a good motor accessory shop can be an enlightening experience, just to show you the sort of things available. Later in this book, you'll find a bit about 'bolt-on goodies', but in this Chapter all we'll concern ourselves with are three items.

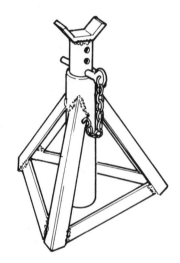

Axle stand

Stroboscopic timing light

The most accurate way of checking ignition timing (that's the time at which the spark occurs) is with the engine running, and for this a stroboscopic (strobe) light is used. This is connected to No 1 spark plug lead and the beam is shone on to the crankshaft pulley mark. Any proprietary light is supplied with full connecting and operating instructions.

Dwell angle meter

This is used for measuring the period of time for which the distributor points remain closed during the ignition cycle of one cylinder, and provides a more accurate method of setting-up the ignition than can be done by simply setting the points gap. Dwell angle meters normally incorporate a tachometer (rev counter if you prefer), which can be useful for

44 checking engine idle speed.

Steel ramp

A Drainer Can in use during an oil change

Cylinder compression gauge

This is very useful for tracing the cause of a fall-off in engine performance. It consists of a pressure gauge and non-return valve, and is simply screwed into a spark plug hole while the engine is turned over on the starter.

Two other useful items are a hydrometer, which is used for checking the specific gravity of the battery electrolyte (this will tell you if you have a dud cell which won't hold a charge), and a 12-volt lamp on a extension lead with crocodile clips which can be connected to the battery terminals.

Care of your tools

Having bought a reasonable set of tools and equipment, it's the easiest thing in the world to abuse them. After use, always wipe off any dirt and grease using a clean, dry cloth before putting them away. Never leave them lying around after they've been used. A simple rack on the garage wall, for things you don't need to carry in the car, is a good idea. Keep all your spanners and the like in a metal box — you can wrap some rags around them to stop them rattling if you're going to carry them in the boot of the car. Any gauges and meters should be carefully put away so that they don't get damaged or rusty. Do take a little care over maintaining your tools too. Screwdriver blades, for example, inevitably lose their keen edges, and a little timely attention with a file won't go amiss.

Service Scene

In the previous chapters, we've discussed the anatomy of your Triumph and outlined the general requirements for keeping it in trim.

Whether you enjoy, tolerate or even dislike motoring, it is for most people the most convenient, and in some cases an essential means of transport. Regular maintenance is of the utmost importance if your car is to provide you with the reliable and economical service it was originally intended to give. It's not until the car suffers a breakdown, or has to spend a day or two in a garage being serviced or repaired, that people appreciate just how convenient a form of transport it is.

The 1300 and 1500 are modern in design, which, if it means nothing else to you, does mean fairly widely spread service intervals and a general reduction in the number of items requiring attention. This has come about from the increased usage of sealed-for-life bearings, nylon bushes, better metal and lubricant technology, and a general reduction in the number of moving parts (which tends to make some owners think their car will go on forever without any regular attention because half the parts don't exist any more!)

Don't be misled, as it's still essential to carry out servicing and inspections periodically in the interests of safety and to gain maximum life from the components, not forgetting the fact that you want to maintain a sensible resale value for your car. The old proverb of prevention rather than cure could never be more appropriately applied than in connection with car servicing. Whether it's a case of casting your eagle eye over the various components critically, or getting stuck into the service tasks in a workmanlike (or workwomanlike) fashion, it's still going to be worthwhile in the end. If you find a worn part, don't ignore it, it won't put itself right. Fix it now and rest assured that it won't let you down at some inconvenient time.

In this Section we've tried to lay out the servicing tasks in such a way that the amount of jacking up etc is reduced to a minimum. The items listed are basically those recommended by the manufacturer plus a few additional ones which we think are well worth the extra effort.

Safety

Before you reach for your tools, let's briefly consider a few precautions. Accidents do happen, this we all know, but the truth is the majority can be avoided if care is exercised. Below we've listed a few points which could reduce the chance of an accident occurring to you, while you're carrying out the service tasks. Many points may seem obvious, and some perhaps you may never have considered.

DON'T run the engine in the garage with the doors closed.

DON'T work in an inspection pit with the engine running.

DO keep long hair, shirt cuffs, ties and the like well clear of any rotating parts while the engine's running.

DON'T grab hold of the ignition HT leads when the engine's running. The chances are you'll get an electric shock, especially if they're dirty or wet.

DO chock the rear wheels when you jack up the front of the car, and vice versa. When you can, also apply the handbrake.

DON'T rely on the car jack when you're underneath. Always use a secondary form of support, eg axle stands, wooden or concrete packing blocks.

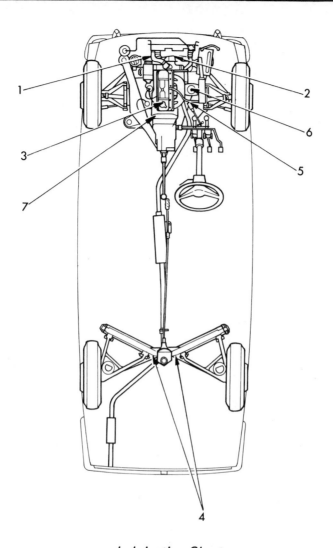

Lubrication Chart

1	Final drive unit	*Hypoid gear oil SAE 90EP*
2	Water pump (where applicable)	*Lithium based general purpose grease*
3	Engine	*SAE 20W/50 multigrade engine oil*
4	Handbrake cable guides and compensator	*Lithium based general purpose grease*
5	Steering gear	*Lithium based general purpose grease*
6	Carburettor dashpot(s)	*SAE 20W/50 multigrade engine oil*
7	Gearbox	*Hypoid gear oil SAE 90EP*

DO wipe up oil or grease from the floor straight away if you should accidentally spill any.

DO get someone to check periodically that everything's OK if you're likely to be spending some time underneath the car.

DON'T use a file without a handle. The pointed tang can easily gash your hand should something go wrong.

DO wear a pair of safety spectacles or goggles to prevent any metal flying into your eyes when using a cold chisel or power tool.

DON'T use your fingers to clear away drilling swarf, a paintbrush is ideal for this job.

DO use the right size spanner for the nut or bolt and see that it's properly fitted before tightening or loosening.

DON'T allow battery acid or terminal corrosion to contact your skin or clothing. If it does, then wash the affected areas with plenty of cold running water.

DO take care when pouring out brake fluid. If you should spill any on the paintwork and it's not removed immediately, it will take the paint off. And do wash your hands afterwards as it's poisonous.

DON'T rush any job, because this is how mistakes are made. If you feel you haven't got enough time to finish the job, don't do it; leave it until tomorrow but don't let this be an excuse for forgetting about it!

Service Schedules

Before we start, just a short comment on time and mileage intervals for servicing. Cars are very similar to people in this respect; if they're inactive they begin to deteriorate, and a car left idle in a garage for a long period needs to have some attention to maintain it in good condition. For this reason the Service Schedules have a time as well as a mileage reference, although we're assuming you use your car fairly regularly and it's not really locked away in the garage for months on end.

One other point worth mentioning is that if you've bought a secondhand car, it's a good idea to give it a full service, regardless of the mileage on the speedometer, and then to plan your service intervals from this first one which you know has been done properly.

WEEKLY, BEFORE A LONG JOURNEY OR EVERY 250 MILES

The following tools, lubricants, etc, are likely to be needed: Tyre pressure gauge, wheel nut brace , lint-free cloth, multigrade engine oil, distilled water, clean tap water, windscreen washer detergent sachet (antifreeze type in winter), cooling system antifreeze/inhibitor, brake/clutch fluid.

1 Check engine oil level (car on level ground)

The engine oil dipstick's on the right-hand side of the engine (viewed from the driver's seat), just behind the carburettor. The check should be made with the engine hot but stationary, so it's best to do it just after a journey. Switch off the engine, and wait a couple of minutes for the oil to drain back into the sump, then pull the dipstick up and out. Wipe it clean with the lint-free cloth and then reinsert it to its full depth; after a few seconds pull it out again and check the level. The difference between the upper 'MAX' mark and lower 'MIN' mark on the dipstick represents about 2 pints (1.14 litres), so use your judgement when you're adding oil to bring it up to the 'MAX' mark; you'll find the oil filler cap at the rear of the rocker cover.

Whatever you do, don't overfill the engine with oil, because it's not only wasteful but can also lead to more expensive engine repairs. Take care with pouring in the oil as you could end up with oil all over the outside as well if you do it too quickly. When you've allowed the oil to drain into the sump (a matter of a couple of minutes), recheck the level and, when you're satisfied the job's completed, make sure that the dipstick and filler cap are properly fitted. Wipe any spilt oil from the engine, and your oil level check's finished.

One other point – if you're using a 5-litre can of oil, you'll probably find it easier to pour the oil into the engine with a small $\frac{1}{2}$ pint can, or a jug or funnel, although some of the cans have plastic spouts, which are quite successful.

2 Check battery electrolyte level

First wipe away any dirt or moisture from the top of the battery, so that none can get inside. Remove the caps, or cover, from the battery cells and check the electrolyte level (with the Lucas Pacemaker battery you can see the fluid level through the battery case). The electrolyte level's correct when the level indicator in each cell is just covered – if your battery doesn't have one, the level should be $\frac{3}{16}$ in to $\frac{3}{8}$ in (5 to 10 mm) above the plates.

Carefully add distilled water to each cell until the level's correct; with the Pacemaker type battery distilled water's poured into the trough until all the rectangular filling slots are full and the bottom of the trough's just covered.

If for some reason you haven't any distilled water, you can use the frost which collects on the walls of the freezer or fridge, and allow this to melt; if you're really desperate, and as a last resort only, boil up some tap water in the kettle and then allow it to cool,

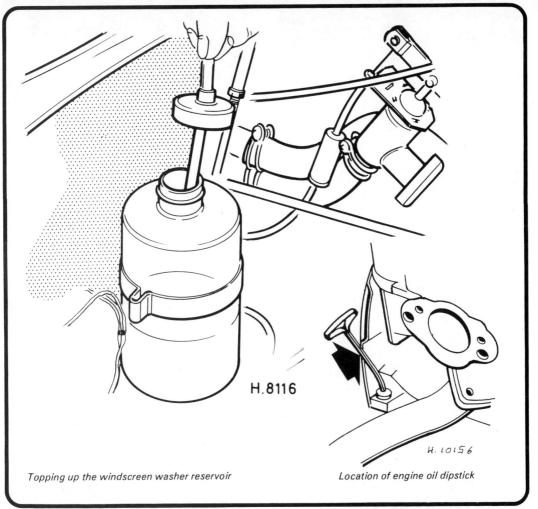

H.8116

H.10156

Topping up the windscreen washer reservoir

Location of engine oil dipstick

Checking battery electrolyte level

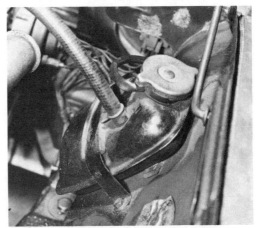

Cooling system overflow bottle (1500 model illustrated)

Checking the tyre pressures

Brake fluid reservoir location

Clutch fluid reservoir location

Sump drain plug

Disposable oil filter cartridge

but don't make a habit of using this or the battery will suffer in the long run.

After topping up the cells, refit the caps or cover, carefully wiping up any drops of water spilt, then check that the terminals are tight. Use two spanners on the terminal bolthead and nut, and there's no need to tighten them very much, just enough to ensure a good contact between the lead terminal and battery terminal; you can easily damage the battery terminal and case if you over tighten them. A very light smear of petroleum jelly can be applied to each terminal to help prevent any corrosion.

If the weather's extremely cold, it's better to top-up your battery before a journey but, if this isn't possible, run the engine for a few minutes after topping-up; this will charge the battery and mix the electrolyte which will prevent the distilled water from freezing.

3 Top up windscreen washer reservoir

Add water as necessary to the windscreen washer reservoir, together with a little of one of the proprietary detergent products for windscreens. In winter, use an antifreeze type (not cooling system antifreeze, because this can damage the car paintwork).

4 Check engine coolant level

Both the 1300 and 1500 models have an overflow reservoir which collects excess coolant from the radiator as the coolant expands with heat. The coolant is drawn back into the radiator when the system cools. The reservoir, which is located on the left-hand side of the engine compartment on the 1300 and on the right-hand side on the 1500, should be kept topped up approximately half full. If the reservoir empties completely it will be necessary to top up the radiator completely full before refilling the reservoir.

It's always best to check the coolant level in the reservoir tank when the engine's cold. Check that the coolant level's about half way up the reservoir tank. If topping up becomes a regular task, you're obviously loosing some coolant which could spell trouble. Causes of loss may be perished or loose hoses, a faulty seal on the pressure cap, a leaking radiator or heater, or a blown cylinder head gasket. If you can't locate the fault then get your local BL Cars agent to carry out a pressure test on the system.

Never remove the pressure cap if the engine's hot; the sudden release of pressure will cause the coolant to boil and you'll get scalded if you're not very careful. If the system's warm, turn the cap very slowly to let the pressure gradually escape, then remove it and top up.

If there's antifreeze in the cooling system and you want to top up the coolant level, you can get away by adding a little water only, but remember you're diluting the antifreeze/water strength so beware, especially in the winter. Further information on draining, flushing and installing antifreeze is given in the 24 000 mile Service Schedule.

5 Check tyre pressures and tread depth

With the tyres cold, check their pressures (see Filling Station Facts for pressure settings). It's always best to use your own pocket-size pressure gauge – those on the forecourts of garages tend to be inaccurate and abused by everyone else but yourself. While you're checking the pressures, don't forget the spare wheel, which should be set at the maximum pressure you're likely to need, then it can be let down if necessary when the wheel's eventually used.

With the tyres now properly inflated run your hands (and eyes) around the tyre walls and tread. This task's best carried out with the car jacked up so that the wheel can be rotated but, if you're really not feeling up to it, move the car backwards or forwards a foot or so, so that you can check all the way round the tyres.

The tread depth must, by law, be not less than 1 mm throughout at least three-quarters of the width, and around its full circumference. Tyre tread depth gauges can be purchased for accurately checking the depth but if you haven't got one a 2p piece can be used. If the tread isn't deeper than the distance from the row of dots to the edge of the coin, you're breaking the law and you'd better get some replacements pretty quickly. There must also be no cuts, bulges or other deformities; if these are present, you're also breaking the law.

If you've got to buy new tyres, read the bit in Save It! but remember it's illegal to fit a radial and a crossply tyre on the same axle, and that radials musn't be fitted to the front if you've got crossplys on the back.

6 Check tightness of wheel nuts

While you're down at floor level, it's a good time to check the tightness of the wheel nuts. Remove the hub caps or wheel caps when fitted, using the flattened end of the wheelbrace (if you've got to use a screwdriver, take care with the chrome and paintwork), and just check that the nuts are tight using the business end of the brace. If your car has cast aluminium wheels fitted, remember that the correct torque is 50% more than a similar steel wheel torque, but even so, there's no need to stand on the wheelbrace. On the subject of aluminium wheels, try not to damage the protective film covering the wheel's outer surface, as this is provided to reduce corrosion. After tightening the wheels, don't forget to **51** refit the hub caps or wheel nut caps properly.

7 Check that all the lights work

Switch on the car lights and check that they're all working correctly. Don't forget to include the direction indicators, brake lights and reversing lights (when fitted) either by getting someone to watch while you operate them or by looking for the tell-tale reflection on the garage wall or adjacent car (shop windows can provide a useful check on brake lights — try it next time you're shopping). If any bulb needs renewing, you'll find the secret of how to get at it in *In An Emergency*. While you're checking the lights, it makes sense to see that the lenses are clean, front and rear.

8 Check the brake and clutch fluid levels

The brake and clutch reservoirs are located on the right-hand side of the engine compartment rear bulkhead; the larger one is the brake reservoir. Remove the reservoir caps and check that the fluid levels coincide with the 'full' line marked on the side of the reservoirs. If necessary top up the reservoirs with Castrol Girling brake fluid, but take great care not to spill any on the paintwork as it has the same effect as paint stripper.

If you find that the reservoir(s) require frequent topping up you have a leakage somewhere in the braking system, which should be attended to by your BL Cars garage immediately for safety's sake.

EVERY 6000 MILES OR 6 MONTHS, WHICHEVER COMES FIRST
(In addition to the items in the weekly/250 miles schedule).

The following tools, lubricants, etc are likely to be needed: Multigrade engine oil, gearbox and final drive unit oil, spark plug spanner, set of feeler gauges, fine emery cloth, timing light, brake adjusting spanner, torque wrench, oil can.

1 Drain the engine oil and renew the filter

Ideally, engine oil changes should only be made when the engine is warm, as this allows the oil to drain out more quickly and take the impurities with it. So, if it is not warm, drive the car for a mile or two — this is better than leaving a cold engine idling because less wear takes place.

Now get a suitable container handy which will just fit beneath the sump. It's got to be fairly shallow, and at the same time have a capacity of at least 8 pints (5 litres); an old plastic washing-up bowl is ideal or perhaps an old 5-litre oil can which has been opened up along one side using a tin opener (mind your hands if you try this!).

Now prepare your self for the dirty part — roll your sleeves up and have some rag ready just in case. Lie on the ground and remove the sump drain plug. You're going to get oil on your fingers, and possibly all over your hand, but if you're quick it won't run right up your arm! If you should happen to drop the sump plug into the container, don't forget it's there — you're going to need it later on. The draining operation will take a good 15 minutes so you can now concentrate on the filter.

You'll need another container to catch the oil in the filter; this holds approximately 1 pint (0.568 litres). In theory you should be able to unscrew (anti-clockwise) the oil filter by hand but in practice you'll probably find it's too tight. This is where the strap wrench makes this task simple but if you haven't got one (they're relatively cheap) you'll have to improvise. One way of doing this is to stab the filter canister with a screwdriver or other sharp tool, and use this as a lever to unscrew it. When you've unscrewed the filter, discard it. Now wipe off the face of the cylinder block, where the filter screws up against it, with a lint-free cloth. Smear a little oil or grease on the rubber sealing ring that's attached to the new filter and screw the filter in until the rubber ring *just touches* the cylinder block face; now turn in two-thirds of a turn further only.

By now the sump should be completely drained, so wipe-around the drain plug hole, check that the copper seating washer's undamaged and refit the plug. Wipe away any oil with the rag. The new oil can be added through the filler cap to bring the level up to the MAX mark on the dipstick. When adding the oil a funnel inserted into the rocker cover will save wasting any, but don't pour the oil in too quickly or the rocker cover will overflow.

Start the engine and run it at a fast idle for about a minute, switch off and allow a further two minutes for the oil to drain back into the sump before rechecking the level, and add more oil as necessary to bring the level up to the MAX mark. Now check the filter and drain plug for leaks; if you've carried out the above instructions carefully there won't be any problem.

There's always a problem when it comes to getting rid of the old oil, you can't just pour it down the household drain because that's illegal as well as anti-social. The local garage might take your waste oil if they've got an arrangement for disposal. If you've bought your oil in a 5-litre can you could put the old oil in there and let the dustman take it away.

2 Check/clean air cleaner element

The air cleaner may be of the renewable paper element type, or metal gauze type. The paper element is normally renewed at intervals of 12 000 miles

(20 000 km) but under very dirty conditions its advisable to renew it more frequently. In any case, the element should be cleaned at 6000 mile (10 000 km) intervals by tapping it gently to remove any loose deposits. Alternatively, use a small brush or low pressure air line (blowing from the *inside* of the element).

On cars fitted with a single carburettor, to remove the paper element detach the rubber tube (when fitted) and undo and remove the two bolts. Lift away the air cleaner. Take off the cover and lift away the element. When refitting make sure the gaskets are correctly located.

On cars with twin carburettors, the twin paper element air cleaner is removed by first undoing and removing the four bolts securing the air cleaner to the carburettors. Lift the assembly clear of the petrol pipe. Remove the bolt, ease off the cover and remove the elements. When refitting make sure that the gaskets are correctly located.

Some cars fitted with a single carburettor may have a gauze element air cleaner, and this must be cleaned every 6000 miles (10 000 km). The element is removed in the same manner as the paper type. It should then be cleaned in petrol, allowed to dry, and then dipped in engine oil, allowing for complete penetration of the oil. Surplus oil is then drained off and the element refitted, ensuring the gasket is fitted the correct way round.

3 Check oil level in carburettor damper(s)

The oil in the upper part of the carburettor acts as a damper for the piston and ensures a smooth and progressive fuel metering. Unscrew the small plastic cap on top of the carburettor and add a little engine oil, if necessary, to bring the level to $\frac{1}{2}$ in (13 mm) for the SU carburettor or $\frac{1}{4}$ in (6 mm) for the Stromberg

carburettor, above the top of the hollow piston rod. Refit the screwed cap; where applicable repeat this for the other carburettor. Carburettor adjustments are covered later in this Schedule.

4 Examine cooling system hoses

Although there may be no loss of engine coolant it's still a good idea to check the condition of the hoses. Press and squeeze them, and check for signs of cracking or perishing. Renew any that appear to be defective. More information on this is given in the 24 000 Schedule covering draining of the coolant and refilling the system.

5 Clean and adjust the spark plugs

The spark plugs play a vital role in the performance and efficiency of the engine, and a little extra care given to servicing them will be well worthwhile. The first thing to do is to remove the plug leads, and if there's any chance of getting them muddled when refitting them, before you pull them off identify them with paint or felt tip pen. Now remove any dirt or grime which happens to be on the surrounding area of each plug with a small brush or cloth, to prevent it from getting into the cylinders. Unscrew the spark plugs with a proper spanner (preferably the type with a rubber insert) but be careful to keep the spanner at the correct angle or you might break the insulator.

Once removed, the plug can tell you quite a lot about the engine condition and carburettor setting, and a note made of this now will help you when you come to adjust the carburettor. If the inner surface of the insulator nose is clean and white, with no deposits on it, you've probably got a weak mixture, provided you've got the correct type of plug fitted. If the insulator nose is covered with hard black looking

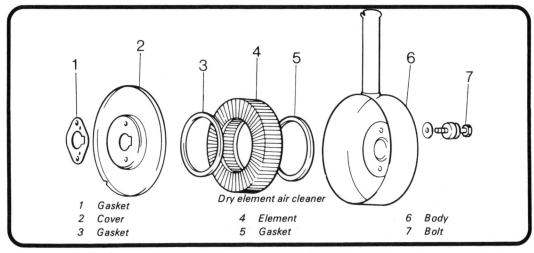

1	Gasket				
2	Cover	4	Element	6	Body
3	Gasket	5	Gasket	7	Bolt

Dry element air cleaner

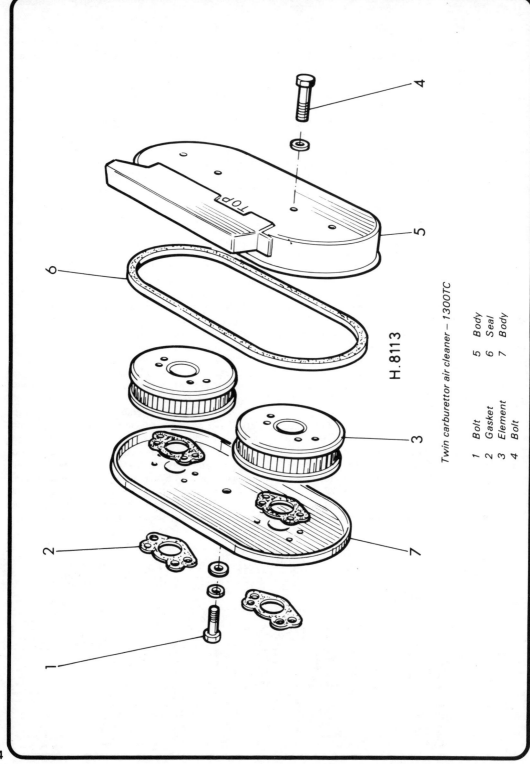

H.8113

Twin carburettor air cleaner – 1300TC

1 Bolt
2 Gasket
3 Element
4 Bolt

5 Body
6 Seal
7 Body

Checking plug gap with feeler gauges

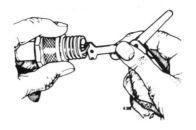

Altering the plug gap. Note use of correct tool

White deposits and damaged porcelain insulation indicating overheating

Broken porcelain insulation due to bent central electrode

Electrodes burnt away due to wrong heat value or chronic pre-ignition (pinking)

Excessive black deposits caused by over-rich mixture or wrong heat value

Mild white deposits and electrode burnt indicating too weak a fuel mixture

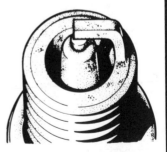

Plug in sound condition with light greyish brown deposits

Spark plug conditions and maintenance

deposits, then the mixture's rich, and if on top of this the surface is oily, the engine's fairly worn and is probably using a lot of oil. A correct mixture setting coupled with an engine in good condition will leave deposits on the insulator nose of light tan to greyish-brown colour. If there are long brown tapering stains on the outside of the plug insulator, the plug's not sealing fully and will have to be renewed.

Although cleaning spark plugs with a wire brush does help, the best method's to sandblast them on a special machine (your local garage may be able to help you), and it's usually possible to give them a compression test at the same time. Any plugs which fail the compression test will have to be discarded. When they're clean, refer to the *Vital Statistics* to find out the correct plug gap for your particular model. Using a set of feeler gauges, check the gap between the plug electrodes, and more often than not it will need adjusting. Bend the *outer* electrode until the feeler gauge is a firm sliding fit; if it happens to be slightly over the correct gap, gently tap the spark plug electrode on something firm like a vice until it's right. If your plugs are the type with a small nut at the top of the insulator, make sure these are tight using a pair of pliers. Now you can refit the plugs, but make sure that the sealing washer's intact first. Screw them in initially by hand, as it's not difficult to cross-thread them and then you'll wish you'd never started the job! Tighten them with the plug spanner (there's no need to overtighten) and then refit the leads. If you've muddled them, No. 1 lead comes from the 9 o'clock position on the distributor cap and is connected to the spark plug nearest the radiator; working in an anti-clockwise direction, the remaining leads are 3, 4 and 2.

6   Check distributor points

Pull off the two clips securing the distributor cap to the distributor body and lift away the cap. Clean it inside and out with a dry cloth. It is unlikely that the four segments will be badly burnt, but if they are, a new cap will have to be fitted.

Push in the carbon brush located in the top of the cap once or twice to make sure that it moves freely.

Gently prise the contact breaker points open to examine the condition of their faces. If they are rough, pitted or very dirty, it will be necessary to renew the contact breaker assembly.

Assuming the points are satisfactory measure the gap between the points by turning the engine over until the fibre (a nylon) heel on the contact set is on the peak of one of the four centre spindle cam lobes.

A 0.015 in (0.381 mm) feeler gauge should now just fit between the points. If the gap varies from this amount slacken off the screw which retains the contact breaker assembly, then insert a screwdriver in

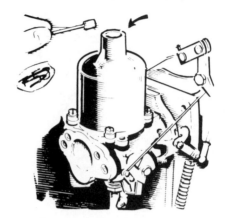

Topping up SU carburettor damper

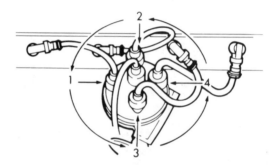

Correct position of HT cables

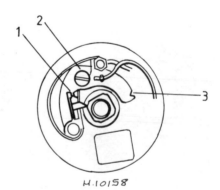

H.10158

Setting the contact breaker points

1   Points gap
2   Retaining screw
3   Gap adjustment notch

the oval notched hole at the end of the plate, turning clockwise to decrease, and anti-clockwise to increase the gap. Tighten the securing screw and check the gap again.

If it is necessary to fit new contact breaker points unscrew the terminal nut and remove it together with the washer under its head. Remove the flanged nylon bush and then the condenser lead and the low tension lead from the terminal pin. Lift off the contact breaker arm and then remove the large fibre washer or second nylon bush from the terminal pin. The adjustable contact breaker plate is removed by unscrewing one holding down screw and removing it, complete with spring and flat washer.

Fitting a new set is a reversal of the removal procedure. Once the new assembly is in place adjust the points as described previously.

Pull off the rotor arm and apply two drops of Castrol GTX to the head of the large screw in the centre of the distributor. This lubricates the shaft bearings. Allow three drops of oil to flow past the base of the cam to the automatic timing mechanism. Smear a faint trace of oil on the cam itself. Apply a tiny spot of oil to the moving contact breaker pivot pin. Too much oil at this point will get onto the points and cause misfiring.

7   Check ignition timing

As the contact breaker heel wears, or where a new set of contacts has been fitted, there may be a slight shift of the ignition timing – that's the exact moment at which the spark occurs at the plugs. Checking the timing statically (that's with the engine stopped) is easily done, and this method is described. If you want the more accurate method, you must use a stroboscopic timing light (this is dynamic timing); the light will come with the necessary operating instructions and you'll find it quite easy to use but, if you haven't got one, it's a job for your local BL Cars garage to do again.

The ignition timing marks comprise a groove cut in one of the apertures of the starter ring cover, located at the front of the engine, and a pointer which is visible through the cover apertures at the 12 o'clock position (see illustration). For the standard 1300 and 1500 models, aligning the groove (C) in the cover with the flat edge of the pointer (B) is the correct position for static timing. However, on the 1300 TC models a 6° BTDC mark is required and can be obtained by first aligning the timing mark (A) and then marking the starter gear cover and its adjacent tooth on the ring gear! Next mark the second tooth up (clockwise when viewed from the front) from the one already marked as shown in the adjacent illustration. This tooth is equal to 6° BTDC and is used as the

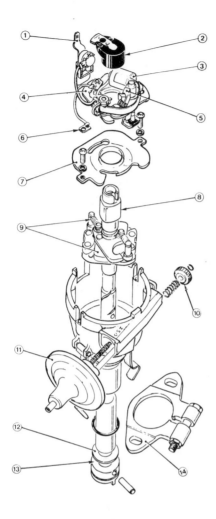

Exploded view of distributor

1   LT terminal
2   Rotor arm
3   Capacitor (condensor)
4   Contact breaker moving plate
5   Contact breaker set
6   Contact breaker earth terminal
7   Contact breaker baseplate
8   Cam
9   Automatic advance springs and weights
10   Vernier adjustment
11   Vacuum advance nut
12   Thrust washer
13   Drive dog and pin
14   Securing plate

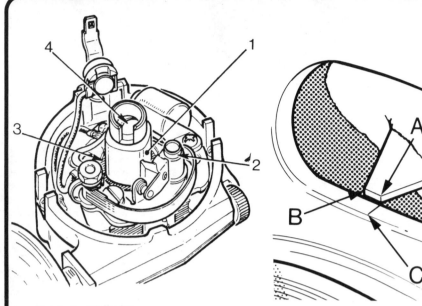

Distributor lubrication

1   Cam
2   Contact breaker pivot
3   Automatic timing mechanism
4   Centre screw

Timing pointer and mark

A – TDC   B – 9° BTDC   C – Timing groove

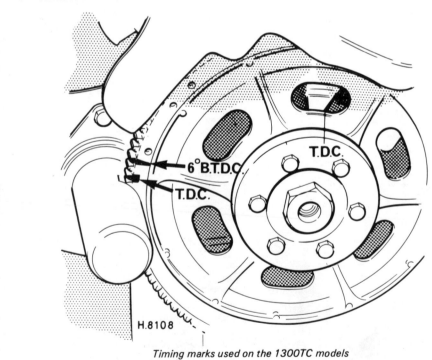

H.8108

Timing marks used on the 1300TC models

static timing mark.

The next task is to remove the rocker cover because you have to make sure that No. 1 piston is in the firing position. Slowly rotate the engine until the timing marks are correctly aligned as described previously. Check that the valves of No. 1 cylinder are closed (there should be clearance between the valve stems and rocker arms). You can double check that you've reached the correct position by taking a look at the valves of No. 4 cylinder which should be both open ('rocking') ie one just opening, the other just about to close. If you find that the valves aren't in this position, rotate the crankshaft a further full 360° and realign the timing marks. When you're satisfied that No. 1 cylinder's on the firing stroke, observe the contact breaker points – they should be just opening. If they're already open, the ignition's advanced (early) and if they aren't about to open the ignition's retarded (late). To adjust the timing, slacken the distributor clamp bolt (it's located at the base of the distributor body) just enough to enable the distributor body to be turned. Having decided whether your ignition timing's advanced or retarded you'll have to turn the distributor body in a clockwise direction to advance it, or vice versa. At the end of this adjustment the contact breaker points should just be on the point of opening, so you can tighten the clamping bolt.

If you find it difficult to judge when the points are about to open, fit up a 12-volt bulb and bulb holder with crocodile clips, and connect one of these to the LT terminal on the distributor and the other to a good earth. With the ignition switched on, turn the crankshaft slowly and the bulb will light just as the points start to open.

Before refitting the rotor arm check that it's not cracked or badly burnt; the same goes for the distributor cap. Inside the distributor cap is a carbon brush contact which should not be damaged; also check that the four pick-up segments aren't burnt and that deposits haven't built up. Finally wipe the distributor cap with a dry cloth both inside and out and refit it, not forgetting the rotor arm.

If you're using a stroboscopic timing light, this is an easier and more accurate way of checking your ignition timing. First of all, it pays to make your timing marks on the starter gear cover and pointer a little more visible by 'highlighting' them with a piece of chalk or dab of white paint; then connect the timing light to the engine in accordance with the manufacturer's instructions. Start the engine and let it idle, but one point that should be made here is that the engine must be at normal operating temperature, otherwise the idle speed could be too fast.

Now carefully disconnect the vacuum pipe from the distributor vacuum capsule and plug the end with a small screw. Point the timing light (which should be flashing) towards the timing marks and check that the setting's right; the timing marks should appear stationary and in correct alignment if it needs adjusting, stop the engine, slacken the distributor clamp, and advance or retard as described above for static timing. Now tighten the clamp and check the setting again with the timing light. Increase the engine speed slowly while still looking at the timing marks, and you should see the timing advance in response to the centrifugal weights in the distributor. With the engine held at a steady speed, get someone to reconnect the vacuum pipe to the distributor; the ignition should advance further as soon as the pipe's connected, and this will indicate that the vacuum capsule's in working order. If you get no response, switch off the engine and check the condition of the vacuum pipe, as sometimes this can be perished or cracked. When you've finished checking the timing, stop the engine, disconnect the timing light, and make sure the vacuum pipe's firmly fitted to the distributor vacuum capsule.

8 Check and adjust valve clearance

The valve adjustments should be made with the engine cold. The importance of correct rocker arm to valve stem clearances cannot be overstressed as they are vital to the performance of the engine. If the clearances are set to open, the efficiency of the engine is reduced because the valves open later and close earlier than was intended. If, on the other hand, the clearances are set too tight there is a danger that the stems will expand upon heating and not allow the valves to close properly, which will cause burning of the valve head and seat and possible warping.

Undo and remove the two holding down studs from the rocker cover, and then lift away the rocker cover and gasket.

Numbering from the front of the engine, valve numbers 1, 4, 5 and 8 are the exhaust valves and numbers 2, 3 6 and 7 are inlet valves.

As it will be necessary to rotate the engine during adjustment of the valve clearances, remove the spark plugs to relieve the compression and find a socket or box spanner which fits the crankshaft pulley nut so it can be used to turn the engine.

It is important that the clearance is set when the tappet of the valve being adjusted, is on the heel of the cam (ie opposite the peak). This can be done by carrying out the adjustments in the following order, which also avoids turning the crankshaft more than necessary.

Adjust valves	Valves fully open
1 and 3	8 and 6
5 and 2	4 and 7
8 and 6	1 and 3
4 and 7	5 and 2

59

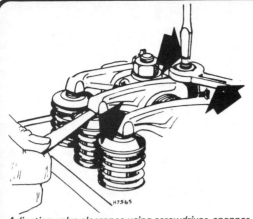

Adjusting valve clearance using screwdriver, spanner and feeler gauge (arrowed)

Dynamo lubrication point

Alternator and dynamo adjustment/mounting bolts

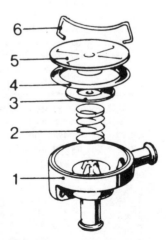

Crankcase breather valve

1   Body
2   Spring
3   Valve plate
4   Diaphragm
5   Cover
6   Clip

The correct valve clearance of 0.010 in (0.25 mm) is obtained by slackening the hexagonal locknut with a spanner while holding the ball pin against rotation with a screwdriver. then, still pressing down with the screwdriver, insert a feeler gauge in the gap between the valve stem head and the rocker arm and adjust the ball pin until the feeler gauge will just move in and out without nipping. Still holding the ball pin in the correct position, tighten the locknut.

9   Crankcase breather valve

To dismantle the valve, disengage the clip and lift out the cover, diaphragm, valve pin and spring. Clean all parts and inspect the diaphragm for damage. If evident obtain a new one. Reassembly is the reverse procedure to removal.

10   Check and adjust fan belt

The fan belt's one of those items a lot of people tend to forget about until it breaks, and then it becomes the centre of abuse. Especially with the amount of motorway use the average car gets today, a little more regular attention to the fan belt will be worthwhile.

Before you adjust the tension have a quick look at the fanbelt, both inside and outside surfaces, turning the engine over by hand if necessary to get a full picture. If you spot any cracks or fraying you can be sure it'll break sooner or later, so it's best to get a new one straight away. To remove the old fan belt, slacken the dynamo or alternator adjustment and pivot bolts, and swivel whichever unit you've got towards the engine as far as it'll go. Slip the old belt over the crankshaft, generator and water pump pulleys and lift it off over the fan blades. Put on the new belt in the same way and then adjust it as follows; the adjustment procedure's the same for new and old fanbelts but you'll need to adjust a new belt again after it's completed about 250 miles.

The fan belt tension's correct when there's $\frac{1}{2}$ inch of lateral movement at the mid-point position of the belt between the dynamo pulley and the water pump pulley. To adjust it, slacken the dynamo or alternator securing bolts and move the unit in or out until the correct tension's obtained. It'll be easier to do this if the bolts are only slackened slightly, so that it requires some force to remove the generator; a long spanner or screwdriver placed behind the unit and resting against the cylinder block serves as a very good lever, and can be held in this position while the adjustment nut is tightened. Tighten the pivot bolts afterwards and check that the tension's correct.

11   Check the battery terminals

Using two spanners on each terminal to avoid stressing the battery, remove both leads and clean away any corrosion with a wire brush; mind your eyes when you're doing this. Use a file to clean up the contact faces of the terminals, and then re-tighten them; don't strain the terminal posts on the battery as you could crack the casing, or worse still, break the terminal post off. Smear each terminal with a small amount of petroleum jelly to help prevent any corrosion. When you're near the battery, check the battery clamp for security, but there's no need to tighten it too much; just enough to keep the battery firm.

12   Lubricate dynamo rear bearing

This will only be necessary on early models fitted with dynamos (it doesn't apply to alternators) and you'll need an oil can to do it. Inject two or three drops of engine oil into the hole marked 'OIL' in the centre of the rear of the dynamo, and wipe any excess oil away with a clean rag.

13 Check condition of steering and front suspension

The first part of this check requires the help of an assistant, so grab a passer-by or borrow your mother-in-law for ten minutes. The weight of the car needs to be on the front wheels, and if you haven't got an inspection pit and are unable to see the steering system properly you'll have to jack the car up and lower it on to some large concrete or wooden blocks. Remember to apply the handbrake and chock the rear wheels, or the car may move.

Now , with your assistant in the driver's seat, get underneath and take a good look at the tie-rod end outer balljoints (the tie-rods are those parts coming out of the steering rack with large rubber convoluted gaiters on them). Ask your assistant to move the steering wheel backwards and forwards until resistance is felt each way, then check for slackness in the tie-rod end balljoints. This will be seen mostly as up-and-down movement if it's there and, if it is, you'll need new tie-rod ends. This is a job for your BL Cars garage or, if you think you're up to doing it yourself, it's all in the Haynes Owner's Workshop Manual for the Triumph 1300/1500.

If there's a knocking noise coming from the steering rack, the chances are it's worn so you should think about getting a replacement rack fitted. Whilst you're taking a look at the steering rack check that the U-bolts are secure – the knocking noise you've heard could be the steering rack sliding to and fro. The convoluted rubber gaiters, at either end of the steering rack are important, if they split or the clips work loose, the lubricating oil in the rack will run out and the rack will wear out prematurely.

Now raise the bonnet and check the condition of the steering column flexible (fabric) and universal joint **61**

Checking the fan belt tension

Removing the brake pad spring clips ...

... and retaining pins ...

... followed by the pads and anti-squeak shims

Rear drum brake assembly on 1500 models

couplings; if wear's found then the defective part should be renewed. Finally check the condition of the steering column bushes by trying to lift the steering wheel up and down; likewise get any worn parts renewed as soon as possible.

To successfully check the condition of the front suspension it's essential to raise the front of the car and support it so that the front wheels are free to hang under their own weight. Now grip the top and bottom of the wheel and try rocking it backwards and forwards in a plane at right angles to the side of the car. If movement is felt and a slight knocking noise is heard, the top and bottom steering balljoints are probably worn. However, before assuming this, check the wheel bearings for wear as described in item 15. If the steering balljoints are worn they should be renewed by your local BL Cars garage as soon as possible. While the front of the car is jacked up, check the condition of the coil springs and shock absorbers.

Don't lower the car to the ground yet as you'll need the front end jacked up to carry out the next checks.

14 Check condition of front disc brake pads

Slacken the wheel nuts and remove the front wheels. If the front wheels are raised clear of the ground and your assistant's still around, get him or her to apply the footbrake while you slacken the wheel nuts otherwise you'll have to lower the car to the ground and then jack it up again.

Take a look at the thickness of the friction material; if it's $\frac{1}{8}$ in (3 mm) or less the pads will have to be removed as detailed below, otherwise refit the roadwheels and carry on to item 15 before you lower the car to the ground.

To remove the disc pads first withdraw the spring clips and pull out the pad retaining pins. The disc pads together with the anti-squeak shims can now be pulled out. Note their position and the directional arrow stamped on the shims for exact refitting. Clean the exposed caliper pistons with a piece of cloth. Before fitting the new pads, it's necessary to press the pistons back into their bores to allow for the extra thickness of the new friction material. When this is done, brake fluid will be forced back into the reservoir, so keep a careful eye on it and either place a cloth under it to catch any overflow or syphon some fluid out (but don't get any in your mouth as it's poisonous).

Press in the pistons squarely and carefully to the bottom of their bores but take care not to damage them – a thinnish piece of hardwood is ideal for the job. Before you begin to fit the new pads it's a good time to check the front wheel bearings for free play as described in item 15. After you've carried out the wheel bearing check, fit the new pads along with the

anti-squeak shims, ensuring that their positions are exactly the same. Now refit the pad retaining pins and the spring clips. You won't have to bleed the brakes after this task but it's essential to pump the footbrake pedal a few times to force the pistons of the calipers out into contact with the new pads. Finally refit the road wheels, lower the car to the ground and check the brake fluid level in the master cylinder reservoir; top it up as necessary.

15 Check front wheel bearings and driveshafts for wear

Wear in the front wheel bearings will usually be indicated by a constant whining noise that will tend to increase with the speed of the car. It should be noted that, if, say, the right-hand side bearing is worn, the noise will decrease when turning a right-hand bend and vice versa. This is because the load on the bearing is altered while the car turns the corner. Bearing wear can also be checked by jacking up the front of the car, gripping the top and bottom of the wheel and trying to rock it backwards and forwards in a plane at right angles to the side of the car. However, any movement that is felt should not be confused with wear in the steering balljoints as described in Section 13.

Wear in the driveshaft constant velocity joints will be indicated by a 'clonk' when the clutch is initially engaged in either first or reverse gear. Also a clicking noise may be heard when the car is driven on full lock. To check the driveshaft, make sure the front wheels are on the ground or ramps with the handbrake applied and then grip each shaft in turn and try and rotate it. A small amount of movement is okay but if the shaft moves excessively the joints will require renewal.

The job of renewing the front wheel bearings and/or driveshafts requires the use of special tools and the job should be entrusted to a skilled mechanic at your local BL Cars garage.

16 Check condition of rear brake linings

Both the 1300 and 1500 models are fitted with drum brakes on the rear wheels. The 1500 brakes are self-adjusting while the 1300 models are manually adjusted by means of a square-headed screw on the rear of the backplate. The method of renewing the shoes for both types is virtually identical and providing the positions of the shoes and springs are carefully noted before removal and reference is made to the adjacent illustrations no major problems should be encountered.

Chock the front wheels, remove the rear wheel hub cap and loosen the wheel nuts. Jack up the rear of the car and place on firm supports to avoid any accidents. Remove the wheel nuts and lift away the **63**

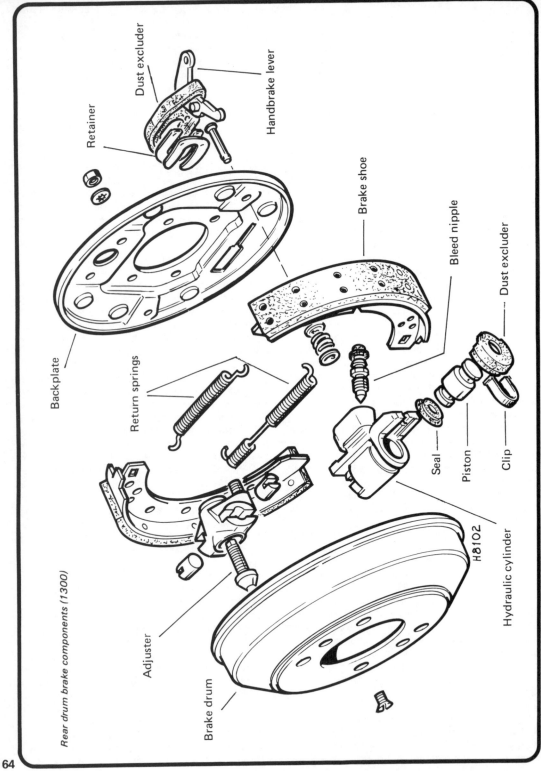

Rear drum brake components (1300)

Dust excluder

Retainer

Handbrake lever

Brake shoe

Bleed nipple

Dust excluder

Backplate

Return springs

Seal

Piston

Clip

H8102

Hydraulic cylinder

Adjuster

Brake drum

64

Rear drum brake adjuster (1300 models)

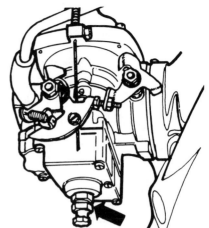

Stromberg carburettor showing jet adjusting nut

road wheel.

Using a wide bladed screwdriver remove the two countersunk head screws, holding the brake drum to the hub. Remove the brake drum. If the brake drum is tight slacken off the brake adjuster (manual type) or carefully prise up the self-adjusting arm and turn the ratchet wheel until it is fully retracted (automatic type). If it will not move away from the hub, use a soft-faced hammer and tap outwards on the circumference rotating the drum whilst completing this operation.

The brake linings should be renewed if they are so worn that the rivet heads are flush with the surface of the lining. If bonded linings are fitted they must be renewed when the lining material has worn down to 0.06 in (1.6 mm) at its thinnest point.

Release the brake shoe web anti-rattle steady spring assembly by first rotating the locking retainer 90° and lifting off the washer, spring and second retainer. Slacken off the brake adjustment if not previously done.

Make a note that the lining on the leading brake shoe is fitted towards the trailing end. Observe the position of the brake shoe return springs, the interrupted spring being at the wheel cylinder end, Also note into which holes the springs locate in the brake shoe web.

To remove the brake shoe lift the trailing end of the shoe from the abutment in the adjuster tappet and the leading end from the wheel cylinder. Unhook the two springs from the shoe web and lift away. It is recommended that strong elastic bands are used to keep the piston in the wheel cylinder.

Thoroughly clean all traces of dust from the shoes, backplates and brake drums using a stiff brush. It is not recommended to use compressed air. Brake dust can cause judder and squeal and therefore it is

important to clean out the brakes thoroughly. Don't inhale the dust – its asbestos content makes it injurious to health.

Check that the piston is free in its cylinder, that the rubber dust covers are undamaged and in position, and that there are no hydraulic fluid leaks. Ensure that the handbrake lever assembly is free and also that the brake adjuster wedge is lubricated with a graphite based penetrating oil.

Prior to reassembly, smear a trace of brake grease to all sliding surfaces and steady posts. Do not allow any grease to come into contact with the linings or rubber parts. Refit the shoes in the reverse sequence to removal, taking care that the two pull-off springs are located in the correct web holes, correctly positioned between the web and backplate. Ensure the shoes register correctly into the slotted ends of the wheel cylinder and adjuster.

On 1500 models, carefully prise up the self-adjusting arm and turn the ratchet wheel until it is fully retracted. In the case of the 1300, slacken off the adjusting screw on the top, rear of the backplate. Now fit the brake drum and retain it with the two screws. Adjust the brakes on the 1300 by screwing in the square-headed adjuster until the brake drum is locked, and then back off the adjuster one or two notches so that the drum turns without binding. To reset the self-adjusting mechanism on 1500 models, apply the handbrake several times until the rear brakes are locked when the lever is raised four or five 'clicks'.

When the brake adjustment is satisfactory refit the road wheels and nuts, lower the car to the ground, tighten the wheel nuts fully and take it for a short test drive.

17 Check and adjust carburettor(s)

Any type of carburettor can only be adjusted **65**

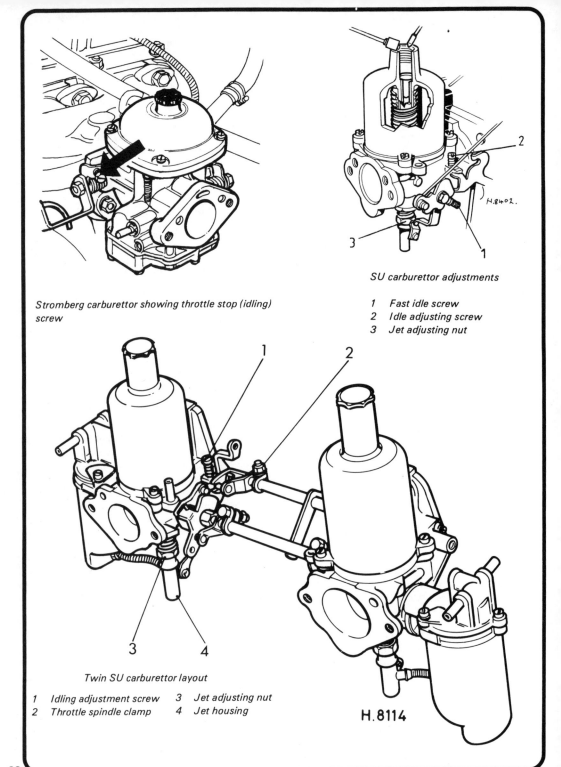

Stromberg carburettor showing throttle stop (idling) screw

SU carburettor adjustments

1   Fast idle screw
2   Idle adjusting screw
3   Jet adjusting nut

Twin SU carburettor layout

1   Idling adjustment screw   3   Jet adjusting nut
2   Throttle spindle clamp   4   Jet housing

H.8114

successfully after the spark plugs, valve clearances, contact breaker points, and ignition timing have been attended to. It's also essential that the carburettor's not worn, and that the engine has reached its normal operating temperature. To accurately set the idling speed it is essential to use a tachometer (see *The Personal Touch*).

Stromberg 150 CD carburettor (1300)

To adjust this carburettor start the engine and run until it reaches normal operating temperature. Stop the engine and remove the air cleaner, damper and clip assembly. Press and hold the piston down with a length of wire held in the oil well so the underside of the piston rests on the bridge of the choke. With a coin, screw up clockwise (when viewed from underneath) the slotted key adjustment nut until the head of the jet can be felt to just touch the underside of the piston. Now turn the jet screw anti-clockwise three full turns.

Start the engine and adjust the idle stop screw so the engine runs fairly smoothly (about 600/650 rpm) without rocking on its mountings. To get the engine to run smoothly at this speed it may be necessary to turn the jet adjustment nut a small amount in either direction.

To check if the correct setting has been found, lift the piston $\frac{1}{32}$ in (0.8 mm) through the air intake with an electrical screwdriver. If the engine speed rises, the mixture is too rich, and if it hesitates or stalls it is too weak. Re-adjust the jet adjusting nut and re-check. Correct setting is obtained when the engine speed does not change when the piston is raised by the required amount.

Single SU carburettor (1500)

Set the engine to run at about 1000 rpm by screwing in the throttle adjusting screw. Check the mixture strength by raising the piston of the carburettor $\frac{1}{32}$ in (0.8 mm) using the piston lifting pin. If the engine speed increases appreciably the mixture is too rich and conversely if the engine speed immediately decreases the mixture is too weak. The mixture is considered correct when the speed rises very slightly.

To enrich the mixture rotate the adjustment nut, which is at the bottom of the underside of the carburettor, in a clockwise direction (when viewed from above), ie downwards. Only turn the adjusting nut a flat at a time and check the mixture strength between each turn. It is probable that there will be a slight increase or decrease in engine speed after the mixture adjustment has been made, so that the throttle idling adjustment screw should now be turned so that the engine idles between 600 and 700 rpm.

Twin SU carburettors (1300 TC)

First ensure that the mixture is correct in each carburettor disconnecting the linkage and adjusting each carburettor as described previously. With a twin SU carburettor installation, not only have the carburettors to be individually set to ensure correct mixture, but also the idling suction must be equal on both. It is best to use a vacuum synchronizing device, from most auto accessory shops. If this is not available, it is possible to obtain fairly accurate synchronization by listening to the hiss made by the air flow into the intake throat of each carburettor. A rubber tube held to the ear is useful for this adjustment.

The aim is to adjust the throttle butterfly disc so that an equal amount of air enters each carburettor. Slacken the throttle shaft clamps on the throttle shaft which connect the two throttle discs together. Listen to the hiss from each carburettor intake and, if a difference in intensity is noticed between them, unscrew the throttle adjusting screw on the other carburettor until the hiss from both the carburettors is the same.

With the vacuum synchronizing device, all that is necessary is to place the instrument over the intake of each carburettor in turn and adjust the adjusting screws until the reading on the gauge is identical for both carburettors.

Tighten the clamps on the interconnecting linkage to connect the two throttle discs of the two carburettors together, at the same time holding down the throttle adjusting screws against their idling stops. Synchronization of the two carburettors is now complete.

18 Check exhaust manifold and downpipe

While you've still got the bonnet open, check the exhaust manifold and downpipe nuts for security. Once the manifold gasket or downpipe connection blows, it's virtually impossible to stop the leak by further tightening as there's usually an accumulation of carbon deposits, so it pays to keep all the manifold nuts secure at all times.

19 Check exhaust system for damage or leaks

With today's stringent laws on motoring, it's worth while making sure that your exhaust system's in good condition. Very often the condition and position of the exhaust mountings play quite an important part in determining the life of the system, and an exhaust which is stressed will undoubtedly have a shorter life than one that isn't. So when you check your exhaust, make a point of seeing whether the mountings are twisted or broken, and renew any that are.

Carry out the check whilst lying on the floor **67**

Gearbox filler/level plug (arrowed)

Final drive unit filler/level plug (arrowed)

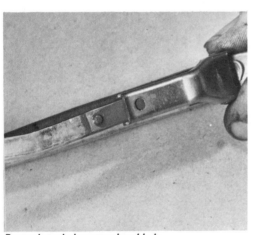

Removing windscreen wiper blade

Removal of windscreen wiper arm

beside the car with the engine running, but, in the interests of safety, make sure the handbrake's fully applied and chock the front and rear wheels substantially. Listen for any escape of exhaust along the whole length. If everything's OK, switch off the engine and make sure the mountings and clamps are secure but, if you find any leaks, get them sorted out by your local BL Cars garage or exhaust specialists, either by welding or renewing.

20 Clutch adjustment

The hydraulic clutch mechanism is self adjusting and no manual adjustment is necessary or provided for.

21 Check gearbox and final drive oil levels

To check the gearbox oil level accurately the car should be on level ground without raising the car. The

gearbox level plug is the upper one; the lower one is the drain plug, and incidentally the gearbox is 'filled for life' so no oil change will normally be necessary unless the oil becomes contaminated or the gearbox is dismantled. Before you unscrew the gearbox level plug wipe the plug and its surrounding area with a rag to prevent any dirt falling into the gearbox when the plug's removed. Now unscrew the plug and if there's enough oil in the gearbox it will just trickle out of the hole. If it's necessary to top up then use an SAE 90EP gear oil. This can be bought in a dispenser with a plastic tube which makes it easy to get the oil into the orifice.

While you're checking the gearbox oil level look for any oil leaks; the quantity of oil you have to add to top up the gearbox will be a good indication of how serious any leakage is.

The final drive unit has a single filler/level plug

and is located in front of the gearbox below the front of the engine. Before unscrewing the plug wipe the plug and its surrounding area with a cloth. Now remove the level plug, and if the oil level's correct it will just trickle over the edge of the hole. If topping up is necessary use an SAE 90 EP gear oil (available in a special dispenser) and add the oil until it just trickles from the lower edge of the filler plug hole. Refit the filler plug.

22 Oil engine controls, door hinges and locks

A few drops of engine oil in the heater and ventilation controls, foot pedals, door hinges and locks will help reduce wear and prevent seizures. After you've worked the oil into the particular joint or whatever, wipe away the excess with a rag; this is most important where door locks are concerned, as women's clothes especially seem to have a natural attraction to oily door locks!

23 Check the lights and seat belts

One of the final jobs – but a most important one still – is to check the operation of all the lights (we've covered bulb renewal in *In an Emergency*) and the seat belts. Make sure seat belt bolts are tightened firmly and, if you have inertia type belts, make sure they function correctly, as your life could depend on them. Frayed or damaged belts should be renewed for the same reason.

24 Check the windscreen wiper arm and blades

The last job's to check the wiper arms and blades for wear. Lift each blade away from the windscreen, and check that the rubber isn't torn or worn, then check each wiper arm pivot for wear and 'sloppiness'. Any part which is worn should be renewed.

To remove the wiper blades, first lift the arm away from the windscreen, then pull the blade spring fastener from the arm whilst disengaging the location 'pip'.

If the wiper arms need renewing, first ensure that they're in the normal 'parked' position. Next undo the small screw at the base of the wiper arm and carefully ease the arm off the splined shaft. If it's obstinate, use a screwdriver to lever it off, but be careful not to damage the splines. When refitting the new arm, make sure it's positioned on the splines so that it parks correctly.

And that's the 6000-mile Service Schedule completed; so treat yourself to a cold beer or kick the dog, depending on your mood!

EVERY 12 000 MILES (20 000 KM) OR 12 MONTHS WHICHEVER COMES FIRST
(In addition to the items listed in the 250 mile and 6000 mile service schedules)

The following tools, lubricants etc will be needed:

Set of spark plugs (4), air cleaner element, petroleum jelly, grease gun, $\frac{1}{8}$ tapered grease nipple, hydrometer.

1 Renew the spark plugs

To maintain optimum engine performance and economy, it's wise to renew the spark plugs regularly at this interval. Use a proper spark plug spanner to do the job, and gap the new plugs with a feeler gauge to the correct clearance for your model; move only the outer electrode to make the adjustment. Make sure the HT leads are secure when you've completed everything.

2 Clean battery terminals and check the specific gravity

If you've got a hydrometer, now's the time to use it to check the battery specific gravity (SG for short). Assuming that it's fully charged, the SG should be as given in the first table according to the battery temperature. If the battery's been on charge, leave it for an hour or two if you can, as it warms up when being charged.

Battery fully charged

SG	Electrolyte temperature
1.268	100°F or 38°C
1.272	90°F or 32°C
1.276	80°F or 27°C
1.280	70°F or 21°C
1.284	60°F or 16°C
1.288	50°F or 10°C
1.292	40°F or 4°C
1.296	30°F or -1.5°C

Battery fully discharged

SG	Electrolyte temperature
1.098	100°F or 38°C
1.102	90°F or 32°C
1.106	80°F or 27°C
1.110	70°F or 21°C
1.114	60°F or 16°C
1.118	50°F or 10°C
1.122	40°F or 4°C
1.126	30°F or -1.5°C

If one cell has a low reading it indicates loss of electrolyte (unlikely unless the casing's cracked) or an internal fault. In either case, the end is in sight so be prepared to purchase a new battery before it lets you down.

From time to time corrosion may appear on the battery terminals or on the ends of the main battery **69**

leads. Where this has occurred detach the battery
leads (negative first), release the clamping plate and
lift out the battery. A solution of warm water and
bicarbonate of soda will remove the corrosion; brush
it on to the terminals, making sure that none gets
inside the cells. Dip the lead ends straight into the
mixture, but too much corrosion will neutralize it so
you may need a second mix. Also clean round the
battery compartment if there's corrosion there too.

During these cleaning operations take care that
the mixture doesn't get into your eyes, as there's a
certain amount of splashing and bubbling as it does
its work. When everything's clean again wipe every
part dry with a clean cloth. An underseal type of paint
can be used in the battery compartment if there's
been corrosion, as this provides a good degree of
protection. Other parts should be smeared with
petroleum jelly before being bolted up. Make sure
everything's covered, but only very lightly. Refit the
battery and connect the leads (positive first), smear-
ing a little more petroleum jelly on to the lead ends
and terminals.

3 Clean fuel pump filter

Unscrew the central retaining screw and lift off
the metal dome cover. Now extract the filter screen
which may have come away with the metal dome or
still be seated on top of the pump body. Remove also
the joint ring. Clean all the parts in petrol, including
the top of the pump, but try to prevent any dirt falling
into the pump itself.

Reposition the filter screen on top of the pump
body and fit the joint ring on top of it. Now refit the
domes cover ensuring the joint ring is correctly
seated. Fit the retaining screw, but take care not to
over-tighten it as the thread is easily stripped.

4 Fit new air filter element

Where a renewable paper element type air
cleaner is fitted, the element(s) should be renewed.
Refer to item 2 of the 6000 mile Service Schedule.

5 Check front driveshafts

Raise the front of the car, support it on axle
stands and check the tightness of the inner driveshaft
coupling bolts. Also check the rubber couplings for
deterioration. If they are worn or perished they should
be renewed by your local BL Cars garage.

6 Grease the steering gear

With the front of the car still raised, locate the
grease nipple on the front of the steering rack
assembly, (see illustration) and apply five strokes of
70 the grease gun filled with Castrol LM grease.

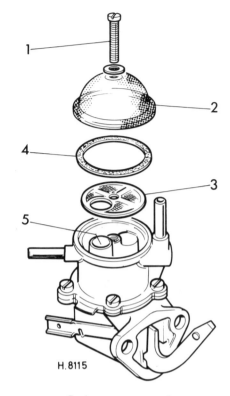

H.8115

Fuel pump components

1	Retaining screw	4	Sealing ring
2	Top cover	5	Valve orifice
3	Filter screen		

Typical driveshaft coupling damage

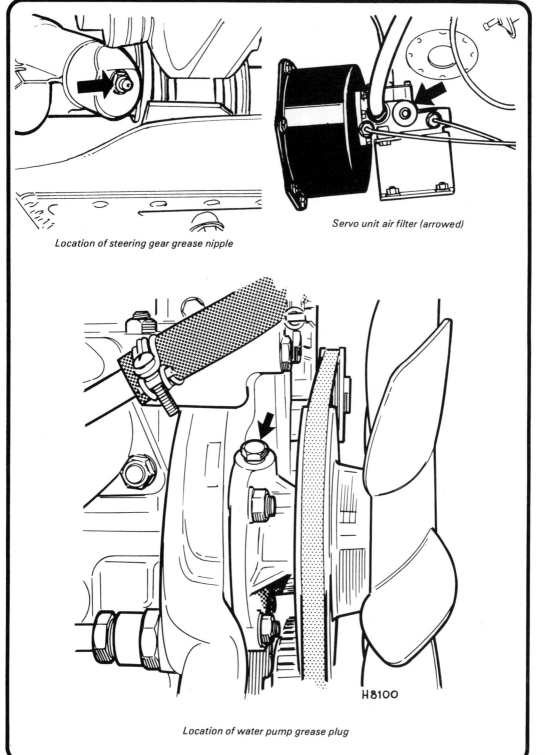

Location of steering gear grease nipple

Servo unit air filter (arrowed)

H 8100

Location of water pump grease plug

7 Grease the water pump bearings (early models only)

While you still have the grease gun handy, remove the blanking plug from the water pump and fit a Briggs tapered grease nipple in its place. Pump in some Castrol LM grease until it starts to come out of the hole in the side of the pump body. You can leave the grease nipple in place of the blanking plug. Later models are fitted with 'lubricated-for-life' water pumps.

8 Renew the brake servo air filter (if fitted)

For the early type servo, undo the air filter cover retaining screw from the side of the servo unit and lift away the cover and filter element. Fit a new filter element and secure it in place with the cover and screw.

Later models require removal of the servo to facilitate renewal of the filter, and this operation should be entrusted to your dealer.

9 Check handbrake pivots for wear and security

Although this is only a check it's as well to lubricate the necessary parts at the same time. Begin at the point where the handbrake cable emerges through the floor of the car (handbrake lever end) and check out the condition and security of the cable. When you come across the yokes and pins check for wear and see that the retaining split pins are in position before lubricating them. Check also the condition of the flexible compensator bracket – if it's deteriorating get it renewed as soon as possible. The same applies to any other parts which show wear.

You can now lower the car to the ground and heave a sigh of relief as that's the 12 000 mile service check successfully completed!

EVERY 24 000 MILES (40 000 KM) OR 2 YEARS, WHICHEVER COMES FIRST
(In addition to the items listed in the 6000 and 12 000 mile Service Schedule)

1 Check brake flexible hoses and hydraulic lines

After checking the brakes, carry out a methodical check of the flexible hoses and hydraulic lines, looking for signs of leaking and damage. In particular you should look for cuts or wear marks on the hoses and rusting or corroding of brake pipes. If you've any doubt in your mind about the safety of anything (and MoT testers are very strict on this subject) let your local BL Cars man check the system thoroughly and renew any pipes as necessary. It's better to be safe than sorry.

2 Change brake hydraulic fluid

The reason for changing the hydraulic fluid in the brake system is that over a period of time the fluid deteriorates. It tends to absorb moisture, and if the water content reaches a sufficiently high level, under hard braking conditions the brakes may fail to operate properly. You'll obviously, therefore, see the importance of changing the fluid. This is a job for your BL Cars garage unless you have sufficient confidence to do this yourself *safely*, as it will involve bleeding the system of air afterwards. In the latter case you'll find the relevant instructions in our Owner's Workshop Manual.

3 Drain and flush cooling system – add antifreeze

The antifreeze should be renewed every two years and the system flushed through to clean out any muck which may be in it.

Begin the draining operation by placing a suitable container under the radiator (something like the plastic washing-up bowl used for draining the engine oil will do), then undo the radiator drain tap (earlier models only) or disconnect the bottom radiator hose (later models). The coolant will start to run out and now, if the radiator cap's removed and the heater control moved to the HOT position, will flow out much faster. When the flow's stopped, open the cylinder block drain tap and drain the block. When all the flow from here has stopped too, get a can of water or a hosepipe, and run water through the system to remove any sediment that might be present. A proprietary flushing compound can be used if you've any suspicions of the system being blocked, but follow the maker's instructions.

When you're satisfied that the system's clean, all hoses in good condition and all connections tight, close the drain tap(s) and reconnect the bottom hose if disconnected, but leave the heat control at HOT. It's not absolutely essential to use antifreeze when refilling the system in warm weather, but it's preferable because it contains special corrosion inhibitors which all good antifreeze has. Antifreeze can stay in the system for two years, and once it's in there's no need to drain it out during the warmer weather. Here's a table which you can use as a guide to how much antifreeze is required.

Antifreeze volume	Protection to	Safe pump circulation
25%	-26°C(-15°F)	-12°C(10°F)
30%	-33°C(-28°F)	-16°C(3°F)
35%	-39°C(-38°F)	-20°C (-4°F)

Having decided how much you need, the

Radiator drain tap

Cylinder block drain tap

antifreeze can be poured straight into the cooling system filler hole followed by enough clean water to fill the system completely. The reservoir expansion tank should be half filled with the same concentration of solution. Refit the caps. Run the engine at a fast idle for a few minutes to let the mixture circulate; as this happens the level may fall as airlocks are displaced, then will fall quite sharply as the thermostat opens. Finally top up the system and expansion tank up to the recommended levels and refit the caps.

Just to check that there are no airlocks, run the car for a short distance, then stop and allow the engine to cool, and recheck the coolant level. Top the overflow reservoir up to the half-way mark as necessary.

EVERY 36 000 MILES (60 000 KM) OR 3 YEARS, WHICHEVER COMES FIRST
(In addition to the items listed in the 6000 and 12 000 mile Service Schedules)

Renew all rubber parts in the hydraulic braking system
This is a job for your local BL Cars garage, or for the enthusiastic owner by following the procedures in our Owner's Workshop Manual. The reason for doing this is that the rubber parts (eg hoses, seals etc) deteriorate after a long period in service. Don't

neglect jobs like this; it's for your safety and everyone else's too.

OTHER REGULAR MAINTENANCE
If you carry out the procedures we've detailed so far, at more or less the prescribed intervals of mileage or time, then you'll have gone a long way towards getting the best out of your Triumph in terms of both performance and long life. That's the good news. The other kind is that there are always other areas, not dealt with in regular servicing schedules, where neglect can spell trouble.

We reckon a bit of extra time spent on your car at the beginning and end of winter will be well repaid in terms of peace of mind and prevention of trouble. The suggested attentions which follow have therefore been divided into Spring and Autumn sections - but there's nothing to prevent you doing them more frequently if you like!

SPRING
We've put this one first as it's less depressing than Autumn – though there's probably more work involved.

Underside of Car
In Spring, we venture to suggest, the owner's fancy lightly turns to thoughts of cleaning off all the accumulated muck of winter from underneath the car. **73**

Without a shadow of doubt, the best time to clean underneath is the worst time from the discomfort point of view — that is, when the car has been driven in the wet and all the dirt is nicely softened up. So let's talk first about the easier way out — steam cleaning or pressure washing. These are not D-I-Y jobs, and can only be done at larger garages, usually those which undertake body repair jobs. You may feel this method is unnecessarily expensive, but it's generally preferable to grovelling about underneath and getting filthy and uncomfortable doing it yourself. However, for the owner who really wants to do it by hand, here goes....

You'll need paraffin or a water-soluble solvent, water (and preferably a hose), a wire brush, a scraper and a stiff-bristle brush. If you think the car floor may leak, remove the carpets or they'll get wet; this will also help you pinpoint the places where water's getting in.

To start with, jack the car up as high as possible, preferably at one side or one end. For your own safety, support it on ramps or concrete or wooden blocks, and chock the wheels that are on the ground; unless both rear wheels are raised, also apply the handbrake.

Now get underneath (you've put it off as long as you can!) and cover the brake discs and calipers with polythene bags to stop mud and water getting into them.

Next loosen any encrusted dirt and, working from one end or one side, scrape or brush this away. The paraffin or solvent can be used where there's oil contamination. After all the brushing and scraping, a final wash down with the hose will remove the last of the dirt and mud.

You can now check for leaks in the floor; if you find any, dry the area carefully then use a mastic type sealer to plug the offending gap. Hollow sections, doors and bodywork can be sprayed or brush-painted with a rust inhibitor to provide some extra protection. If there are signs of the underseal breaking away, this is a good opportunity to patch it up. Undersealing paint is available in spray cans or tins from accessory shops; one small point about putting the stuff on though, and that's to make sure the area is clean and dry, otherwise you're wasting your time.

While you're underneath, have a good look round for signs of rusting. Likely places are body sills, floor panels, lower sections of the front wings, and main chassis channel sections, particularly by the rear suspension arm anchorage points. If you do find rust, have a word with the local BL Cars agent or body repair shop before things get too bad.

Bodywork

This too will have suffered from all the muck and salt that's around during the winter, and there's no better time to wash it thoroughly and check for stone chips and rust spots. You're bound to find some despite the regular washing you've given the car — or meant to — throughout the winter. Treat as for rusty scratches (see *Body Beautiful*).

After the touch-up paint has thoroughly hardened, it's worth giving the car a good polish to prepare it for the long, hot summer ahead (well there's no harm in hoping). If you're feeling really energetic you could do the interior as well (*Body Beautiful* again) but the most important cleaning jobs are done now.

AUTUMN

With winter on the way, your car's electrical system, for example, is going to take much more of a beating than it has during the last few months. Now — and not on a dark night miles from anywhere in a snowstorm — is the time to check the vital components. Where other Sections or Chapters are referred to in brackets, the detailed procedure's described there.

Battery

Ensure that it's topped up correctly (*Weekly Schedule*)
Check and clean as necessary (*12 000 mile Service Schedule*)

Fan Belt

Check condition and tension (*6000 mile Service Schedule*)

Lights

Check operation (*Weekly Schedule*)
Renew any failed bulbs (*In an Emergency*) or check for faults as necessary (*Troubleshooter 6*).

Wipers/Washer

These are going to get a lot of use so check the wiper arms and blades (*6000 mile Service Schedule*). Top up the washer reservoir (*Weekly Schedule*) and check operation.

Cooling System

Check all hoses (*6000 mile Service Schedule*).
Drain, flush and refill system with new antifreeze mixture if necessary (*24 000 mile Service Schedule*).

Tyres

Check tread and condition (*Weekly Schedule*). Remember that you may well have to drive in slippery conditions.

Bodywork

Finally, if you've got any energy left, wash the car and polish it thoroughly to help protect the paint against the winter elements.

Body Beautiful

If you've bought this book intending to do all the routine servicing of your car yourself, then you'll surely want to keep the bodywork and inside of the car looking good too. And for anyone who doesn't here's how to do it anyway ...

It's always a good idea to clean the interior first; this way you won't get the dust all over your nicely polished exterior – or the car's! Begin by removing all the contents, not forgetting the odds and ends in the pockets and glovebox. Then take out all the mats and carpets, which should be shaken and brushed, or better still vacuum-cleaned. If they need further cleaning this can be done with a carpet shampoo, but let them dry thoroughly before you put them back. Any underfelt should be taken out and shaken, too, but don't try washing this or it may end up in rather more pieces than you started with.

If the carpets should just happen to be in such a bad state of decay that they don't merit cleaning, why not get yourself a decent set of replacements? You can get kits tailored for your particular model from specialist firms, and they're quite reasonably priced.

The inside of the car can now be cleaned with a brush and dustpan, or again preferably a vacuum-cleaner. If the flex on the Hoover won't stretch to the car (and the car won't squeeze through the front door!) it might be worth thinking about investing in one of the small 12 volt hand vacuums which can be attached to your car battery – your accessory shop can probably show you one.

Seat and trim materials can be wiped over with warm water containing a little washing-up liquid, but for best results (particularly if they're very dirty) use one of the proprietary upholstery cleaners, which are specially made for the job. An old nail brush will help to remove ingrained marks, but don't splash too much water about and do wipe the surfaces dry afterwards with a clean cloth, leaving the windows open to speed up drying. The carpets can be put back when they're quite dry, making sure they're properly fitted around the controls etc.

You have to be careful about cleaning car windows, especially the windscreen, with some household products as these can leave a smeary film. Water containing a few drops of ammonia is probably best, but any stubborn marks and smears can be removed with methylated spirit; finish off with a chamois leather squeezed as dry as possible.

Just in case you should think that's it, there's still the boot to be dealt with. Take out that collection of junk that seems to have grown every time you open the lid, and get busy with brush or vacuum cleaner again. While you're at it, if you must carry all that stuff around, now's the time to try and stow it so it doesn't rattle any more!

Now you can pause for a moment – make a well earned cup of tea perhaps – and take a critical look at the interior. Are there any nicks or tears in the seats or other trim? Is the headlining drooping or peeling? Some excellent products can now be obtained for repairs such as these. One of the most useful is probably the vinyl repair kit, which comes in various colours and consists of a quantity of 'liquid vinyl' and some sheets of texturing material. The liquid is applied to a split or hole in a plastic seat or piece of trim, smoothed like body filler, and allowed to set. It's then blended into the surrounding area by selecting the best matching pattern from the graining material supplied, placing this over the repair and rubbing with a hot iron; the pattern is then embossed in the repaired area. This type of repair's equally successful, **75** incidentally, on vinyl roofs if your car happens to have one.

For larger splits or tears it may be necessary to cut a piece of matching material from somewhere that doesn't show, apply some suitable adhesive to it and work it under the edges of the tear, pressing these together as neatly as possible once the glue has become tacky enough. Any loose headlining or trim can also be stuck in place – but make sure you get an adhesive that's suitable for PVC or vinyl.

Once you've got the seats in a reasonable state of cleanliness and repair, why not consider seat covers? Like the carpets, they're available from specialist firms to suit your car and are a worthwhile buy in view of the protection they give.

If you use your car regularly and you've got the time and inclination, it should really be washed every week, either by hand (preferably using a hosepipe) or by taking advantage of the local car-wash if there is one. Whichever method you choose (assuming you wash your car at all!) we don't think we need tell you how to do it – but remember it's never a good idea to just wipe over a very dirty car, whether wet or dry; you might as well sandpaper it!

Two or three times a year (even once is better than not at all) a good silicone or wax polish can be used on the paintwork. We don't know which of the many makes you'll use, so we can only recommend you to follow the maker's instructions closely so that

you do see a reward for your efforts. Chrome parts are best cleaned with a special chrome cleaner; ordinary metal polish will attack the finish.

If the paint's beginning to lose its gloss or colour, and ordinary polishing doesn't seem to help, it will be worth considering the use of a polish with a mild 'cutting' action to remove what is, in effect, a surface layer of dead paint. Your friendly neighbourhood accessory shop man will advise on a suitable type.

The remainder of this Chapter describes how to keep your car's bodywork and paintwork in good condition by dealing with scratches and more major damage too, as they occur. A number of repair aids and materials are referred to, most of them essential if you're to achieve good results. They should all be available, together with free advice, from good motor accessory shops.

Keeping paintwork up to scratch

With superficial scratches (the sort only other people seem to get) where they don't penetrate down to the metal, you'll be glad to hear that repair can be very simple. Lightly rub the area with a paintwork renovator or a fine cutting paste to remove any loose paint from the scratch and to clean off any polish. Rinse the area with plenty of clean water and allow to dry. Apply touch-up paint to the scratch using a fine brush, and continue to build up the paint by several

Likely rusting points on the Triumph 1300/1500 range

applications, allowing each to dry, until it's level with the surrounding area. Allow the new paint at least two weeks to harden (knitting or a crossword puzzle will help to pass the time), then use the paintwork renovator or cutting paste again to blend it into the original. Now a good polish can be used.

For anyone who's as lazy as we are, the easy alternative to painting over a scratch is to use a 'paint transfer', available in packs to match popular car colours. Prepare the affected area in the same way as for touch-up paint, then simply pick a transfer of a suitable size to cover the scratch completely. Hold the transfer against the area and burnish its backing paper, and if you're doing it right you should find it sticks to the car paintwork (rather than your hand), and at the same time frees itself from the backing. The patched area can now be polished to blend it in.

When you've got a scratch that's penetrated right through to the metal, causing rusting, you need a different technique. Use your Scout knife to remove any loose rust from the bottom of the scratch, then paint on a rust-inhibiting paint to prevent it from spreading. You'll probably now need to apply cellulose body stopper paste – use a rubber or nylon applicator or a knife, but don't borrow one from the kitchen as you'll have a job cleaning it!

The paste can be thinned down if necessary using cellulose thinners. Before it hardens, it's a good idea to wrap a piece of smooth cotton rag round the end of your finger, dip it in thinners and quickly sweep it across the filled scratch. This ensures that the area is very slightly hollowed and allows the paint to be built up to the correct level as described earlier.

Dealing with dents

When your car's bodywork gets a deep depression, you'll probably have one too. But there's no reason why even fairly large dents can't be tackled successfully by the D-I-Y owner, especially using the excellent body repair materials now available. So cheer up, and let's see what can be done.

The first step is to try to pull the dented metal out to bring it more or less back to the original level. Don't expect to make a perfect job of this – you won't; the metal has stretched and 'work-hardened' which makes it a virtually impossible job. Try to bring the level up to about $\frac{1}{8}$ inch below the surrounding area; obviously, with shallow dents you can bypass this bit. If the underside of the dent can be got at, try hammering it out gently from behind, using a hammer with a wooden or plastic head. You'll need to hold a fairly heavy hardwood block on the outside of the dent; this absorbs the impact of the hammer blows and helps to stop the metal being dented in the opposite direction!

If you've got a dent in a completely enclosed body section, or there's something else preventing you from getting behind it, a different approach is needed. Try to screw up enough courage to drill several small holes through the metal in the dent, particularly in the deeper parts. Now screw in several self-tapping screws so that they get a good bite, and either pull on the heads with pliers or wrap some heavy gauge steel wire round them and pull this. Brace yourself in case something gives suddenly or you may dent your own bodywork!

Now to remove the paint from the damaged area. This is best done using a power drill and abrasive disc, but if you've got the time and energy you can use elbow-grease and abrasive paper. Don't forget to remove the paint from an inch or so of the surrounding good paintwork, too, so that everything blends in nicely. Now score the metal surface with a screwdriver or the tang of a file to provide a good key for the filler which you're going to have to apply, in case you didn't know. Now, to finish off the repair, refer to the filling and spraying section at the end of this Chapter.

Rust holes and gashes

If there's any paint left on the affected area, remove it as described above so that you can get a good idea of just how bad the problem is. If there's more rust or fresh air than good metal, now's the time to consider whether a replacement panel would be more appropriate; this is a body shop job beyond the scope of this book.

If things don't seem that bad and you're prepared to have a go at doing the job yourself, remove all the fittings from the surrounding area except those which may help to give a good guide to what the shape should be (e.g. headlamp shells). Now, get a hacksaw blade or a pair of snips and cut out all the loose and badly affected metal. Hammer the edges inwards so that you've got a recessed area to build up on.

Wire brush the edges to remove any powdery rust, then paint over with a rust inhibitor; if you can get to the back, do the same to that. You're now going to fill the hole with something, but unfortunately just anything won't do. The best bets are zinc gauze, aluminium tape or polyurethane foam. The gauze is probably the favourite for a large hole. Cut a piece slightly larger than the hole to be filled, then position it in the hole so that its edges are below the level of the surrounding bodywork. If necessary, hold it in place with a few blobs of filler paste. For small or narrow holes you can use the aluminium tape which is sold by the roll. Pull off a piece and trim to the approximate size and shape required. If there's backing paper, peel it off (it sticks better that way) and place the tape over the hole; if necessary, pieces can be overlapped at the edges. Burnish down the **77**

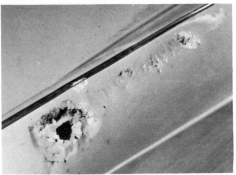

The procedure given with these photos is simplified; more comprehensive instructions will be found in the accompanying text. Typical rust damage is shown here, but the procedure for the repair of dents and gashes is similar.

First remove fittings from the immediate area and then remove loose rust and paint. A wire brush or abrasive disc mounted in a power drill is best, although the job can be done by hand. You need to be very thorough.

The edges of a hole should be tapped inwards with a hammer to provide a hollow for the filler. Having done this, apply rust inhibitor to the affected area (including the underside where possible) and allow this to dry thoroughly.

Before attempting to fill larger holes, block them off with suitable material. Metal tape can be used, but the picture shows a piece of aluminium gauze being sized up for use on this hole.

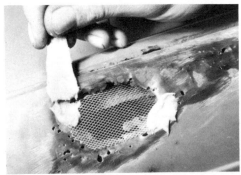

When mixing the body filler, follow the manufacturers' instructions very carefully. Mix thoroughly, don't mix too much at one go, and don't make it up until you're ready to start filling – modern fillers begin to harden very quickly!

The tape or gauze used for backing up a hole can be secured in position with a few small blobs of filler paste. It's a good idea to mix a very small quantity for this purpose first.

After mixing the filler, apply it quickly with a flexible applicator, following the contours of the body. The filler should be built up in successive thin layers, the final one being just above the level of the surrounding bodywork.

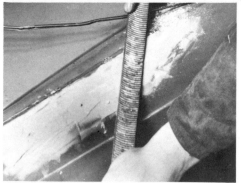

A fairly coarse file or cutting tool is best for removing excess filler and for achieving the initial contour. Care must be taken not to overdo the filing or you'll hollow out the surface and have to fill it again!

A sanding block will now be needed; this can be made of wood as shown or a purpose-made rubber one can be purchased. Begin shaping the filler by using the block with progressively finer grades of dry abrasive paper, followed by ...

... wet and-dry paper, keeping both the work area and the paper wet. Rubbing down is complete when the filled area is 'feathered' into the surrounding painted areas, as shown; this final stage is achieved with the finest grade paper.

After thorough washing and drying, any necessary masking can be done and a coat of primer applied. Again, build this up with successive thin layers. Once the primer is dry it should be smoothed with very fine wet-and-dry paper.

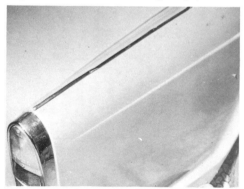

The top coat of paint can now be applied, again in thin layers. Later a mild cutting paste can be used to blend it with the surrounding paint. Finish off with a good quality polish.

edges of the tape with a file handle or similar to make sure it's firmly adhering to the metal.

Polyurethane foam is best used in hollow body sections but, if you're using this, follow the maker's instructions carefully. When this foam hardens it can be cut back to just below the level of the surrounding bodywork with a hacksaw blade.

With the hole now blocked off, the affected area can be filled and sprayed as follows.

Filling and spraying

Many types of body filler are available, but generally speaking those proprietary kits which contain filler paste (or filler powder and resin liquid) and a separate hardener are best. You'll also need a flexible plastic or nylon applicator (usually supplied) for putting the mixture on with. Mix up a little of the filler on a piece of board or plastic (those plastic margarine tubs are ideal but do wash out all traces of the contents first!). Read the instructions carefully and don't make up too much at one go. You'll find you have to work fairly fast or the mixture will begin to set, especially if you've been a bit generous with the hardener.

Apply the paste to the prepared hole or dent more or less to the correct level and contour, but don't try to shape it once it's become tacky or it'll pick up on the applicator. Layers should be built up at intervals until the final level's just proud of the surrounding bodywork.

When the filler has fully hardened, use a Surform plane or coarse file to remove the excess and obtain the final shape. Then follow with progressively finer grades of wet-or-dry abrasive paper starting with coarse, followed by medium, then fine (some manufacturers give 'grit' grades to their wet-or-dry paper – 40 is the coarsest, 400 the finest). Always wrap the paper round a flat block if you're trying to get a flat surface, and keep it wet by rinsing in clean water or the filler and paint will clog up the abrasive surface.

At this point, the doctored area should be surrounded by a ring of bare metal, encircled by a feathered edge of good paintwork. Rinse it with plenty of clean water to get rid of all the paint and filler dust, and allow it to dry completely.

If you're happy with the surface you've obtained, then you're ready to apply some paint. First spray over the whole area with a light coat of grey primer. This will show up any surface imperfections which may need further treatment, and will also help you get the knack of spraying with an aerosol can before you start on the colour coats. Rub down the surface again, and if necessary use a little body stopper, as

80 described for minor scratches, to fill any small

imperfections. Repeat this spray-and-level procedure until you're satisfied with the finish; then wash down again and allow to dry.

The next stage is to apply the finishing coats, but first a word or two about the techniques involved. Paint spraying should be done in a warm, dry, windless, dust-free atmosphere – conditions not very readily available to most of us! You may be able to approach them artificially if you've got a large indoor workshop, but if you have to work outside you'll need to pick the day carefully. If you're working in your garage you'll probably need to 'lay' the dust on the floor by damping it with water.

If the body repair's confined to a small patch, mask off the surrounding area to protect it from paint spray. Bodywork fitting (chrome strips, door handles and the like) will need to be either masked or removed. If you're masking, use genuine masking tape and plenty of newspaper as necessary. Before starting to spray, shake the aerosol can thoroughly; then experiment on something (an old tin or similar will do – not the neighbours' car!) until you feel you can apply the paint smoothly. At the previous stage this wasn't too important, but now you're trying to get the best possible finish.

First cover the repair area with a thick coat of primer – not as one coat, but built up of several thin ones. When this is dry, using the finest wet-or-dry paper, rub down the surface until it's really smooth. Use plenty of water to keep the surface clean; when it's dry, spray on another primer coat and repeat the procedure.

Now for the top coat. Again the idea's to build up the paint thickness by several thin coats. Have a test spray first as this is a different aerosol, then commence spraying in the centre of the repair area. Using a circular motion, work gradually outwards towards the edges until the whole of the repair and about two inches of the surrounding original paint is covered. Remove all the masking material 10 to 15 minutes after you've finished spraying.

Now you can start putting away all the bits and pieces because it'll need about two weeks for the paint to harden completely. After this time, using a paint renovator or a very fine cutting paste, blend the edges of the new paint into the original. Finally, apply a good wax or silicone polish, and hopefully you'll have a repair you're proud to own up to!

Adding 'Pinstripes'

There are various kinds of self-adhesive body decor available for customising your car. Perhaps the neatest and most suitable of the 'add-on' variety are 'Pinstripes', and we've mentioned these here as they may appeal to the owner who wants a cheap and simple way to improve the appearance of his or her car. They're an adhesive tape which comes in different widths and colours, and as single or multi-stripes. Most have a backing paper which is peeled off as the stripe's applied.

When applying any of these self-adhesive tapes, first make sure the paintwork's clean by washing with warm water and a car shampoo or liquid detergent. Next clean up the surface with a very fine cutting paste or paintwork renovator, and wash down again. You can now apply the tape, but follow the directions carefully. Smooth it down with clean rag and, if necessary, prick out any small air bubbles with a pin. Try not to stretch the stripes as you put them on because they'll shrink slightly anyway; and wrap the ends round the panels so that they don't pull away at the edges.

The Personal Touch

On the subject of accessories it's been said that, if someone makes it, the motorist will buy it. The 'after-market' in extras and accessories has now grown to enormous proportions; you only need to browse through a car magazine or motor accessory shop to see what we mean. The problem for any motorist is to sort out the useful and practical items from what, at the other end of the scale, is some undoubted rubbish.

The subject of accessories is so broad that in a Handbook like this we can only 'touch the tip of the iceberg' so we've tried to cover just a few of the more popular accessories and to include some tips on fitting where appropriate.

All good products will be supplied with general fitting instructions which may or may not require minor modifications to suit your Triumph. If you're buying secondhand however, you may not get any fitting instructions at all. The guidelines given here aren't intended to replace those given by the manufacturer, and if you're in doubt about fitting a particular item, they're the people to refer to.

NOTE: always disconnect the battery before commencing any work involving the electrical system. Fireworks are very pretty, but there's a time and place for everything!

Auxiliary instruments

It would be quite easy to fill a whole book just on the subject of auxiliary instruments and how to fit them but, as with other things, you'll probably get pretty good instructions when you buy them. Because the Triumph 1300 and 1500 are already fitted with an ammeter and temperature gauge as standard, we're only going to consider battery condition indicators, clocks, oil pressure gauges, tachometers, and vacuum gauges.

First of all, even before you've decided what instruments you're going to fit, you've got to decide where to fit them. The dashboard of the 1300 or 1500 doesn't lend itself readily to fitting brackets and small extra panels, because the instruments will end up by being rather low down and will obstruct your view forward if fitted to the top of the dashboard. Some instruments such as tachometers can be 'pod' types, which can be mounted to the top of the dashboard. The other answer may be a console mounting, which will not only allow you to fit instruments but may have a radio installation compartment and/or a storage pocket too. Some information on these is given later.

Sooner or later you're going to have to start drilling some holes somewhere, but this shouldn't cause you any problems if it's approached in the right way. First of all make sure that there's nothing behind the panel before even considering drilling a hole, and that there's enough room to fit the instrument, switch, or whatever, in the space chosen. Any hole which will have a cable or capillary tube running through it must have a plastic or rubber grommet to prevent the metal cutting through; these grommets can be obtained from D-I-Y accessory or car electrical shops.

When it comes to drilling larger holes for instruments, start off by centre-punching the centre of the area, then use compasses or dividers to mark the hole, allowing a little for clearance (standard instruments are 2 in/52 mm diameter). It's best to mark another hole inside the first hole, and drill around this line so that the centre part can be pushed out; if you're using a $\frac{1}{8}$ in drill the inner circle will need to be $\frac{1}{16}$ in inside the first circle marked. Finish the job

Some of the supplementary instruments and accessories available from Smiths Industries

off by carefully filing and deburring the hole.

Battery condition indicator

The battery condition indicator's simply a voltmeter, and as such must be connected to a good earth point on the chassis and to any suitable connection which is live when the ignition is 'ON'. For convenience this could be the switched terminal on the ignition switch. You won't need heavy cables for the battery condition indicator, 14/0·30 (14/0·012) should be OK, but make sure that the earth polarity's correct. *Note: The 1500 models are fitted with a battery condition indicator as standard.*

Clock

Clocks come in many forms; you can even get car clocks powered by dry cell batteries. Most car clocks which are wired to the car's power source contain semi-conductors. If this means nothing else to you, it should mean that there's a negligible load on the battery and that the polarity's critical if you don't want to cause permanent damage. Connections are much the same as the battery condition indicator except that you don't want the clock to stop when the ignition's switched off. Therefore connect the feed wire to a fuse which is permanently live.

Tachometer

The tachometer (rev counter) is the one instrument that's available in larger sizes than the others (80 mm instead of 52 mm, although the smaller sizes can be obtained). Most are positive *or* negative earth, but you must connect them up correctly. In case you should pick up a secondhand one, connections for the most common types are shown in the illustrations. Note that with the Smiths types, the distributor-to-coil LT lead is removed; also note the sleeve colours on the main white lead. Use a 14/0·30 (14/0·012) cable size.

Oil pressure gauge

Oil pressure gauges may have a sender unit or a capillary tube in much the same way as the water temperature gauge (although the instruments are very different). Here you can use a T-piece and connect it into the oil pressure switch tapping which is above the oil filter on the left of the engine. For the electrical type, connections are similar to those described for the water temperature gauge.

Vacuum gauge

Also called a performance gauge or fuel consumption gauge, this is simply a suction (negative pressure) gauge with a flexible connection that screws into a tapping on the inlet manifold. The idea is to drive at all times with the highest possible vacuum reading, and once you get the knack of it, it can save you quite a bit in petrol.

Consoles

Consoles come in all shapes, sizes and prices. Before buying, have a good look round to see what's on the market – that includes looking through the motoring D-I-Y magazines. Some types extend back from the engine compartment wall or dashboard to behind the handbrake, the handbrake and gear levers coming up through the console base panel. You can get them with cut-outs for switches, radios and tape players, and for the standard 52 mm diameter circular instruments. Many types also have an ashtray or storage pocket, some also have an armrest; there's even a type that fits to the roof! They come in a variety of finishes – black leatherette, fibreglass, woodgrain, and in various colours. Without a great deal of difficulty you should be able to get something that suits both your taste and your pocket.

Fitting's usually straightforward, but you may need to drill a few holes which could lead to your buying some self-tapping screws as well. Before drilling, don't forget to look what's on the other side of the panel, or your console could prove rather expensive!

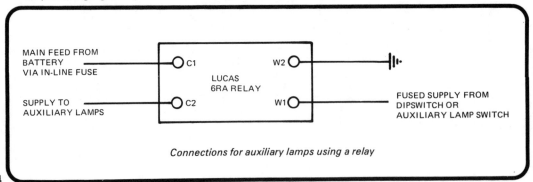

Connections for auxiliary lamps using a relay

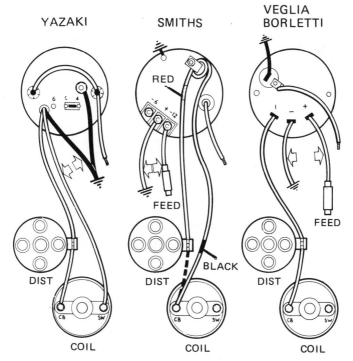

YAZAKI SMITHS VEGLIA BORLETTI

RED

FEED

BLACK

FEED

DIST DIST DIST

COIL COIL COIL

Connections for three popular tachometers

Yazaki: *Negative earth shown – reverse arrowed wires to change polarity*

Smiths: *Positive earth shown – the dotted connection must be removed when the tachometer is fitted*

Veglia Borletti: *Negative earth shown – reverse arrowed wires to change polarity*

Warning devices

Air Horns

Air horns are marketed by several companies as a D-I-Y installation kit comprising the horns themselves, a compressor unit, a relay, plastic piping and electrical cable. What you've obviously got to do is mount the horns reasonably near the compressor, and the compressor reasonably near the relay, or the connections just won't reach. It's normal for the manufacturers to specify a certain way up for the compressor to be mounted, but there shouldn't be any other problems. You'll need to make sure that the electrical connections are as power the makers' instructions for the relay and compressor, and decide whether you want to use the air horns in conjunction with, or in place of, the original car horn. If you have to connect into existing wiring, make sure the connections are well made and, if these involve soldering, don't forget to insulate any soldered joints.

Hazard warning

It's to be hoped that you'll never break down on a busy road or in an awkward spot, but if it does happen then it's reassuring to have a hazard warning system fitted. This is a device which enables all four direction indicator lamps to flash simultaneously to warn other vehicles that you're stationary and to help them spot you in bad visibility – not (despite frequent use for the purpose) to indicate that you've parked on double yellow lines to pop into the tobacconists!

Full instructions will be supplied with the kit, but wiring can be a bit tricky as there are a number of connections to be made into existing circuits.

Child safety seats and harnesses

Much has been said in recent years about the use of seat belts for front seat passengers, and more recently there's been an increasing interest in the various special rear seats and harnesses now available for young children. It's very difficult to give **85**

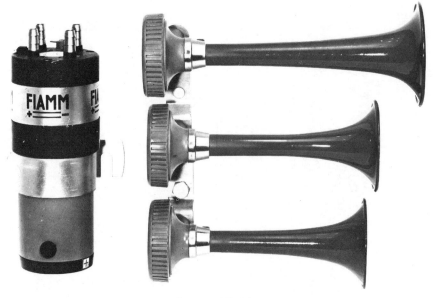

Fiamm 'trio' air horns

any precise instructions for fitting these, because there are so many types around, but what you must be careful about is ensuring that you buy a BSI-approved type.

Most types have a pair of straps at the lower edge which need to be attached to the rear seat pan at the back of the squab, and a further pair of straps that fit over the back of the car seat for attachment to the rear parcel shelf. Take very careful note of the manufacturers' instructions; they require the anchorages to be a certain distance apart, and may also require reinforcing plates to be used.

Before starting to drill holes for the mountings, make sure that the underside or rear of the panel's clear of obstructions, pipes or any other components. It may also be possible to utilise existing tapped fitting points. If you're in doubt, get in touch with the seat or harness manufacturers – they'll be only too pleased to give advice.

Auxiliary lamps

When auxiliary lamps are fitted, not only must you fit them in a suitable place on the car, but that place must also meet certain legal requirements; where these apply we've attempted to give some guidelines.

In addition to the actual lights themselves, we have to think of the switches (not normally difficult **86** because many small switch panels are available, or you may already have a console which will take them, or you can simply drill a hole in a suitable spot on the dash panel), fusing, cable sizes, and whether relays are necessary.

Spot and fog lamps

It's illegal to mount these with their centres *more than* 3 ft 6in (1067 mm) from the ground. Any lamps that are mounted with their centres *less than* 2 ft (610 mm) above the ground may only be used in fog or falling snow, and a single lamp may be used only *in conjunction with* headlamps. The lamps must always be mounted and used in pairs, two fog, two spot, or one of each if they're to be used independently of the headlights. Their inner edges must be *not less than* 13·8 in (350 mm) apart and their outer edges must be *within* 15¾ in (400 mm) of the edge of the car. If they're used as spotlamps, they must conform to the normal anti-dazzle requirements, by wiring them via the dipswitch or by pointing them slightly downwards.

Choose the lamps carefully, and if possible match the lamp styles. There are many good types on sale, so if you're not sure what you want seek some advice. The actual mounting's not too difficult; probably the best method on the Triumph is to suspend them beneath the bumper by fixing to the bumper brackets.

To prevent overload of the switch or wiring, a relay should be used (the Lucas 6RA type, part no.

33213 is suitable). This is connected through the switch from the existing headlamp circuit to one of the relay 'coil' terminals, the other going to a good earth point. The lamp wires then go to one of the relay 'contact' terminals with the other terminal going either to the battery or the battery terminal on the starter solenoid via an in-line fuse. The fuse rating will depend on the lamp manufacturers' recommendations, but will probably be about 20 amps for bothlamps. A good place to mount the relay is fairly near the starter solenoid or battery, to reduce the cable runs to a minimum.

Reversing lamps

Provision's made for a reversing light switch in the gearbox housing; this is a standard BL Cars part and is much preferable to any dashboard mounted type. Cable from the switch should be run through the car floor if possible and under the carpet, but don't forget to use grommets or the holes which you've drilled will cut through the cable insulation.

You utilise the existing reversing light apertures and lenses provided in the rear light cluster, and all you'll have to buy is the switch, wire, bulb holders and bulbs. Alternatively you could purchase some flush-mounted lamps but obviously these will cost you more than the previous suggested method.

Remember that if you don't fit a gearbox operated switch, any other type you use will have to have a warning light wired in parallel with the reverse light. An in-line fuse will also be required, probably about 10 amps rating, but it will depend on the actual lamp(s) used.

Rear fog lights

These can often be mounted in much the same way as the separate reversing lamps, although bumper-mounting types are very popular. For wiring, the same sort of instructions apply as for separately switched reversing lamps (in fact some types serve a dual function in having a clear lens for reversing and a red snap-on lens for the fog lights).

Anti-theft devices

There are three main categories of car thieves — those people who want your car either as a complete item or for the major mechanical and body parts, those who are out for a joy-ride; and those who merely want the contents. With any type of thief it makes sense to do what you can to deter someone from *wanting* to get in; don't leave valuables lying about, don't leave the car unlocked and, if it's parked at home, put it in a locked garage if possible. But, if a car thief decides he does want your particular car, statistically he's got a pretty good chance of getting it!

The 1500 models have a steering column lock which is a very effective protection against a car being driven away, but it still makes sense to have a good burglar alarm fitted. Many types are available, and many of these are wired into door courtesy light switches or hidden switches beneath seats. Other types are wired into the horn circuit, but separate horns and bells are available; the more unconventional it is (whilst still being reliable!), the better. Don't put hidden switches in the first place you think of — it might be the first place the thief thinks of too.

Some anti-theft devices are activated by the movement caused through somebody trying to get into the car (and occasionally by an innocent passer-by!). Some not only sound alarms, but also earth the ignition circuit; other devices simply mechanically lock together the steering wheel and brake pedal. Have a look round the accessory shops and see what suits your car, your pocket and the degree of protection required.

Visibility aids

Mirrors

Recent EEC legislation has done wonders for the looks of exterior mirrors. In addition to being functional, they now must have no projections to catch clothing or other cars, and must fold flat when struck. The result is a new wave of products in all shapes and sizes, some of which can be sprayed to match up with the existing car finish. There has also been a marked swing recently from wing mirrors to the door-mounting kind. Choose mirrors which you think will suit the car's styling, and having got them, select the mounting point carefully. You'll get a good idea of where the best place is by simply looking at other cars, but get someone to hold the mirror while you sit in the driving seat just to make sure you can see all you need to, and make sure too that the quarter-light will still open.

When fitting this type of mirror, you'll need to mark the hole position, then do likewise for the other side. Some door mirrors have a bolt type of fixing, which will mean removing the trim panel; others are simply attached by self-tapping screws. For the larger holes, check the size needed and, if you can, select a drill this size, plus, where applicable, a smaller one to make a pilot hole. If you haven't got a large enough drill, you'll have to drill one or more smaller holes and file out to the correct size. Don't forget to remove any burrs from the hole afterwards, then apply a little primer to cover the bare metal edges. When the primer's dry you can fit the mirror following the makers' instructions, then swivel it to get the best rear view.

For mirrors which only need self-tapping screws, make sure the drill used for the holes isn't too big. Ideally it should be fractionally larger than the thread root diameter – it's better to make sure that the hole's on the small side and enlarge it if necessary, rather than start off with a hole that too big for the screws to bite properly.

Rear window demisters

At one time, if your car wasn't fitted with a heated rear window as standard equipment (and only the expensive models were) about the only remedy was a stick-on clear panel designed to act a bit like double glazing. They didn't usually work very well and frequently came unstuck too. Now they've been more or less superseded by the element type of stick-on demister. These act more like the genuine article, consisting of a metal foil element which is peeled off a backing sheet and stuck on to the inside surface of the rear window glass. It has to be wired up to the electrical system, of course, via a suitable fuse and switch, using sufficiently heavy cable and preferably incorporating a warning lamp, as it will take quite a large current and shouldn't be left on inadvertently. The great thing about these devices is that they do work, and are very moderately priced.

Headlamp conversions

Still on the subject of better visibility, if your problem's seeing in the dark then you might well consider uprating your headlamps. A number of conversions are available for 1300/1500 models, and mostly they're fitted by simply interchanging with the old ones, no wiring modifications being needed (see *In An Emergency* for headlight removal).

Radios and tape players

A radio or tape player is an expensive item to buy, and will only give its best performance if fitted properly. It's uselss to expect concert hall performance from a unit that is suspended from the dash panel by string with its speaker resting on the back seat or parcel shelf! If you don't wish to do the installation yourself there are many in-car entertainment specialists who can do the fitting for you.

Make sure the unit purchased is of the same polarity as the car, or that units with adjustable polarity are correctly set before commencing installation.

It's difficult to give specific information with regard to fitting, as final positioning of the radio-tape player speakers and aerial is entirely a matter of personal preference. However, the following paragraphs give guidelines to follow, which are relevant to all installations.

Radios

Most radios are a standardised size of 7 inches wide, by 2 inches deep – this ensures that they'll fit into the radio aperture provided in many cars. The following points should be borne in mind before deciding exactly where to fit the unit:

MAG 'European' door mirror

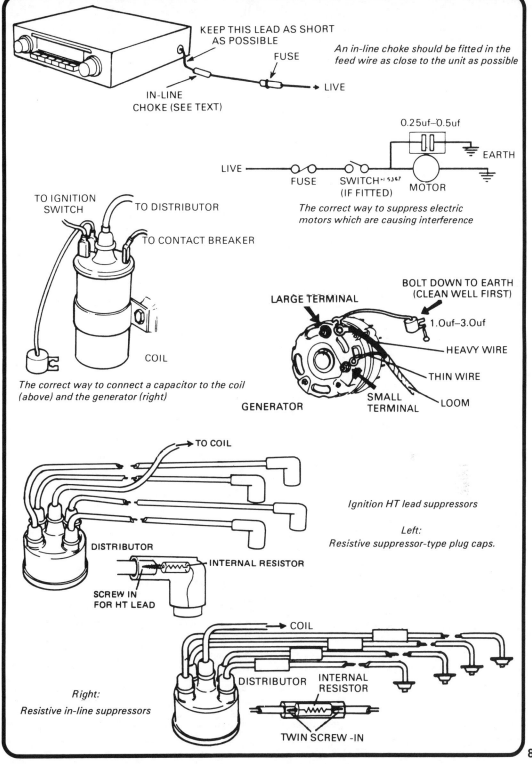

KEEP THIS LEAD AS SHORT AS POSSIBLE

FUSE

An in-line choke should be fitted in the feed wire as close to the unit as possible

IN-LINE CHOKE (SEE TEXT)

LIVE

0.25uf–0.5uf

EARTH

LIVE

FUSE

SWITCH (IF FITTED)

MOTOR

The correct way to suppress electric motors which are causing interference

TO IGNITION SWITCH

TO DISTRIBUTOR

TO CONTACT BREAKER

COIL

BOLT DOWN TO EARTH (CLEAN WELL FIRST)

LARGE TERMINAL

1.0uf–3.0uf

HEAVY WIRE

THIN WIRE

LOOM

GENERATOR

SMALL TERMINAL

The correct way to connect a capacitor to the coil (above) and the generator (right)

TO COIL

DISTRIBUTOR

INTERNAL RESISTOR

SCREW IN FOR HT LEAD

Ignition HT lead suppressors

Left:
Resistive suppressor-type plug caps.

COIL

DISTRIBUTOR

INTERNAL RESISTOR

Right:
Resistive in-line suppressors

TWIN SCREW -IN

(a) *The unit should be within easy reach of the driver wearing a seat belt*

(b) *The unit shouldn't be mounted close to an electric tachometer, the ignition switch and its wiring, or the flasher unit and associated wiring*

(c) *The unit should be mounted within reach of the aerial lead, and in such a place that the aerial lead won't have to be routed near the components detailed in 'b'*

(d) *The unit shouldn't be positioned in a place where it might cause injury to the car occupants in an accident; for instance, under the dashpanel above the driver's or passenger's legs*

(e) *The unit should be fitted really securely*

The type of aerial used, and where you're going to fit it, is a matter of personal preference. In general, the taller the aerial, the better the reception but there are limits to what's practicable. If you can, fit a fully retractable type – it saves an awful lot of problems with vandals and car-wash equipment. When choosing a suitable spot for the aerial, remember the following points:

(a) *The aerial lead should be as short as possible*

(b) *The aerial should be mounted as far away from the distributor and HT leads as possible*

(c) *The part of the aerial which protrudes beneath the mounting point musn't foul the roadwheels, or anything else*

(d) *If possible the aerial should be positioned so that the coaxial lead doesn't have to be routed through the engine compartment*

(e) *The aerial should be mounted at a more-or-less vertical angle*

Radio interference suppression

Books have been written on the subject, so we're not going to be able to tell you a lot in this small space. To reduce the possibility of your radio picking up unwanted interference, an in-line choke should be fitted in the feed wire and the set itself must be earthed really securely. The next step is to start connecting capacitors to reduce the amount of interference being generated by the different circuits of the car's electrics. When it comes to the ignition HT leads, there are resistors which can either be suppressor-type plug caps or in-line suppressors; if you're already using resistive HT leads (those with the carbofibre filling), they're already doing the job for you.

Tape players

Fitting instructions for both cartridge and cassette stereo tape players are the same and in general the same rules apply as when fitting a radio.

Tape players are not usually prone to electrical interference like radios – although it can occur – so positioning is not so critical. If possible the player should be mounted on an 'even-keel'. Also, it must be possible for a driver wearing a seat belt to reach the unit in order to change, or turn over, tapes.

Comfort

Sound reducing kits

Longer journeys can be more pleasant if your car's comfortable to drive, and a couple of suggestions on this theme may be welcome.

Very few cars have yet been produced in which the noise level, particularly at motorway speed, is all that could be desired. For economy reasons, most manufacturers put only a certain amount of underfelt and sound-deadening material into their cars, and a further improvement can usually be made by fitting one of the proprietary kits. These are usually tailored to fit individual models, and consist of sections of felt-like material which are glued in place under carpets, inside hollow sections, boot lid etc., in accordance with instructions. The material can also be bought in rolls for D-I-Y cutting, using the carpets etc, as templates.

Seats

If your seats are showing signs of old age, (and new covers won't disguise the sagging, when you sit in them), then you can of course have them rebuilt by an upholstery specialist. On the other hand, if you think that the seats in the Triumph models aren't the most comfortable ever made, you could think about replacing at least the driver's seat by one of the special bucket-types available. To look at these you'll need to find an accessory shop stocking the more motor sport orientated kind of goods.

Miscellaneous

Electronic ignition

Such systems are many and varied and most are widely advertised. The makers claim easier starting, better performance and lower fuel consumption as the main advantages, and on the whole these claims are substantiated in practice. However, before buying one of the available kits we suggest you stop and reflect whether your mileage and type of driving makes the expenditure worthwhile. Get other advice, preferably from someone who's fitted such a system to his own car. Consider too, whether you're capable of installing it yourself, otherwise you'll have to pay for fitting as well.

There are several types of electronic ignition – some retain the conventional contact breaker in the car's distributor while others replace this by a

Desmo's ingenious 'Accordion' roof rack folds up to fit in the boot when not in use

magnetic triggering device. Even where the contact points are retained they're no longer likely to burn and therefore shouldn't need renewing very frequently — but this doesn't in itself amount to much of a a saving.

Wide wheels

With increasing petrol and insurance costs, and decreasing speed limits, many motorists have stopped trying to get the ultimate in performance from a given engine size and drifted towards other things. One of these things, which not only smartens up the car, but can improve the roadholding considerably, is a set of wide wheels.

You can get steel wide wheels, which are usually less than half the price of a new radial tyre, but most people like the looks of the light alloy ones. Practically all the popular types are made from the LM25 aluminium alloy; prices vary, but typically they'll cost you a little more than the tyre that goes with them. For anyone who really wants to spend some money (and there can't really be any justification for it for normal road use) there are the magnesium alloy types; these will set you back about twice as much as the aluminium ones.

There was a time when all light alloy wheels had a bad reputation, but this seems to have improved considerably with the more modern casting techniques. They can still be porous, which could mean that you'll need a tube with the tyre if you're going to keep the air in, but they're normally sealed during manufacture to help overcome this.

The wheels need to be treated with a little more care than steel wheels. To prevent corrosion setting in it's important to keep them clean, particularly if there's salt on the roads, and to re-lacquer them from time to time. Don't hit kerbs; a steel wheel may only suffer a dented rim but you can easily knock a piece out of a light alloy rim and that's the end of that.

When you're having tyres fitted, extra care must be taken to prevent the rim being damaged, and it won't go amiss if you remind the tyre fitter at the time. Any balancing weights must be of the stuck-on-type, not the ordinary clip-round-the-rim type. The tyres themselves must be suitable for the rims, and because there are so many types around you'll have to take some advice from the wheel and tyre supplier. You'll also have to consult him for advice on the widest wheel size that can be used without resorting to tin-bashing around the wheel arches.

Steering wheels

One of the most popular, easily fitted accessories is a special steering wheel. Many types are available, but often it's also necessary to buy a boss which fits on to the steering column shaft, to which the steering wheel's attached. No problems should be encountered when fitting a steering wheel or boss,

once the old wheel's been removed.

First of all ensure that the front wheels are pointing straight ahead, then carefully prise out the centre motif. Remove the screws securing the horn bar to the contact plate and lift away the horn bar. Pull out the little horn brush and put it in a safe place. Grasp the steering wheel with one hand, to prevent it turning and use a $\frac{7}{8}$ in AF (22 mm) or 1 in AF socket (depending on the model) to undo the centre nut. Don't remove the nut, leave it screwed on a couple of threads and then strike the steering wheel evenly from behind with the palms of your hands to release it. Hopefully the steering wheel will separate itself from the splines of the steering column (and if you left the nut on a few threads as we suggested the steering wheel won't have hit you in the face as it came away!).

Refitting of the replacement steering wheel must not be in accordance with the manufacturer's instruction which probably will be a direct reversal of the removal procedure for the old wheel.

Roof racks

It's not surprising that many an owner has to resort to a luggage rack from time to time, even if it's only for family holidays. The types available are very varied, but they normally rely on clips attached to the water drain channel above the doors. If you're buying, select a size that suits your requirements, making sure that it's not too wide for the roof!

When fitting the roof rack, position it squarely on the roof, preferably towards the front rather than the rear. After it's loaded by the way, recheck the tension of the attachment bracket screws.

Don't keep the roof rack on when it's not wanted; it offers too much wind resistance and creates a surprising amount of noise (see *Save It!*).

Mudflaps

You're probably already aware that both front and rear wheel arches can be fitted with mudflaps. These will not only protect your car's underside and paintwork from flying stones, but will also earn the thanks of following drivers owing to the reduction in spray during wet weather. Fitting's straightforward and is usually by means of clamping brackets or self-tapping screws.

Specialist Fitments

We've now covered a lot of the main items likely to interest the average owner from the D-I-Y fitting angle. Such things as towbars and sunshine or vinyl roofs, while practical or desirable, are beyond the scope both of this book and of the ordinary car owner. We therefore recommend that for any major accessory of this kind you consult the appropriate specialist who'll be able to give you an initial estimate of the cost as well as carrying out the work properly and safely.

Troubleshooting

We've gone to great lengths in the Handbook to provide as much information on your car as we think you'll need for satisfactory running and servicing. Hopefully, you won't need to use this Chapter but there's always a possibility (rather than a probability!) that something will go wrong, and by reference to the charts you should be able to pinpoint the trouble even if you can't actually fix it yourself.

The charts are broken down into the main systems of the car, and where there's a fairly straightforward remedy – the sort you can tackle yourself – **bold type** is used to highlight it. Further information on that particular item will normally be found elsewhere in the book; look up the component or system in the Index to find the correct page. In some cases a reference number will be found (eg T1/1); by looking up this number in the accompanying Cross-Reference Table, you'll find more information on that particular fault.

TROUBLESHOOTER 1:

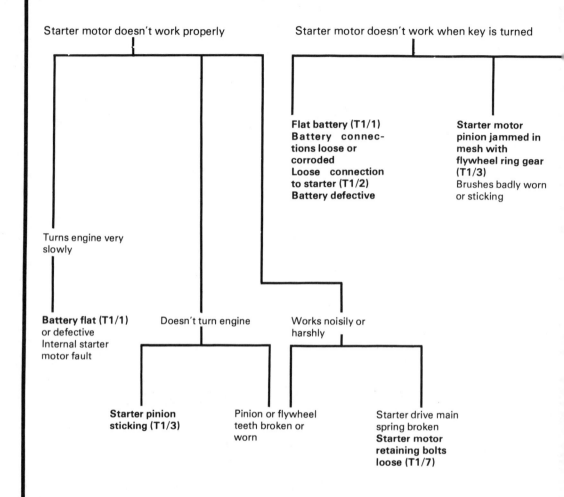

Starter motor doesn't work properly

Starter motor doesn't work when key is turned

**Flat battery (T1/1)
Battery connec-
tions loose or
corroded
Loose connection
to starter (T1/2)
Battery defective**

**Starter motor
pinion jammed in
mesh with
flywheel ring gear
(T1/3)**
Brushes badly worn
or sticking

Turns engine very
slowly

Battery flat (T1/1)
or defective
Internal starter
motor fault

Doesn't turn engine

Works noisily or
harshly

**Starter pinion
sticking (T1/3)**

Pinion or flywheel
teeth broken or
worn

Starter drive main
spring broken
**Starter motor
retaining bolts
loose (T1/7)**

ENGINE – STARTING

Starter motor turns engine normally but engine won't start

Ignition system fault

Fuel system fault

Other causes

Starter motor or solenoid switch faulty internally

Air cleaner blocked
Valve clearances incorrect
Inlet manifold or gasket or carburettor gasket leaking
Brake servo hose leaking (if fitted) **(T1/8)**
Engine seriously overheated (T1/9)

Spark plug lead(s) loose, disconnected or damp (T1/4)
Spark plugs dirty, cracked or incorrectly gapped
Distributor or coil cap cracked or HT lead loose
Worn distributor cap electrodes
Coil or condenser faulty (T1/5)
Contact breaker points dirty or incorrectly set
Ignition timing incorrect

Fuel pump faulty filter blocked (T1/6) or cable disconnected
Leak in fuel pump or fuel lines
Carburettor float chamber fuel level(s) incorrect
Carburettor incorrectly adjusted
Choke not operating correctly

TROUBLESHOOTER 2:

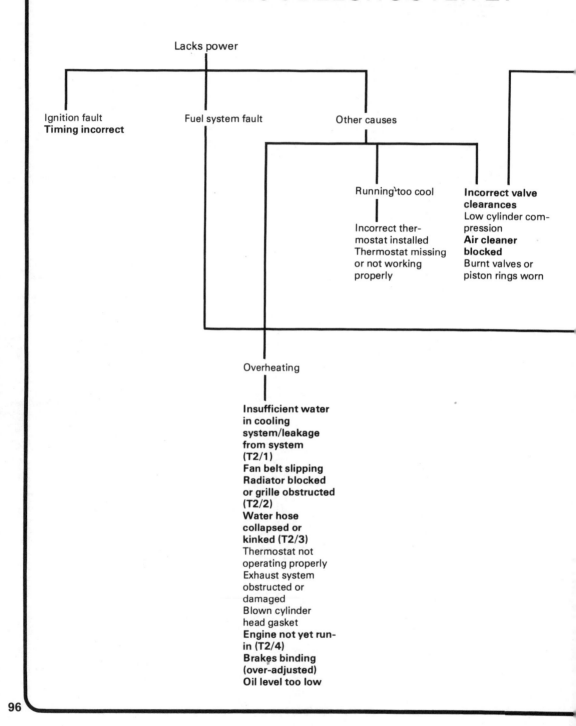

Lacks power

Ignition fault
Timing incorrect

Fuel system fault

Other causes

Running too cool

Incorrect ther-
mostat installed
Thermostat missing
or not working
properly

**Incorrect valve
clearances**
Low cylinder com-
pression
**Air cleaner
blocked**
Burnt valves or
piston rings worn

Overheating

**Insufficient water
in cooling
system/leakage
from system
(T2/1)
Fan belt slipping
Radiator blocked
or grille obstructed
(T2/2)
Water hose
collapsed or
kinked (T2/3)**
Thermostat not
operating properly
Exhaust system
obstructed or
damaged
Blown cylinder
head gasket
**Engine not yet run-
in (T2/4)
Brakes binding
(over-adjusted)
Oil level too low**

ENGINE – RUNNING

Misfires

Cuts out unexpectedly

Ignition fault

Fuel system fault

Ignition fault

Fuel system fault

**Water on ignition components (T1/4)
Coil or condenser faulty (T1/5)
LT lead to coil or distributor disconnected (T1/4)
HT lead from coil loose or disconnected (T1/4)**

**Tank empty
Fuel pump faulty, lead disconnected or filter blocked (T1/6)**
Fuel line broken, leaking or blocked

**Spark plug lead(s) loose, disconnected or damp (T1/4)
Spark plugs dirty, cracked or incorrectly gapped
Distributor or coil cap cracked or HT lead loose
Worn distributor cap electrodes
Coil or condenser faulty (T1/5)
Contact breaker points dirty or incorrectly set
Ignition timing incorrect**

Fuel pump faulty, **filter blocked (T1/6) or cable disconnected**
Leak in fuel pump or fuel lines
Carburettor jet blocked
Carburettor float chamber fuel line(s) incorrect
Carburettor incorrectly adjusted
Choke not operating correctly

TROUBLESHOOTER 3:

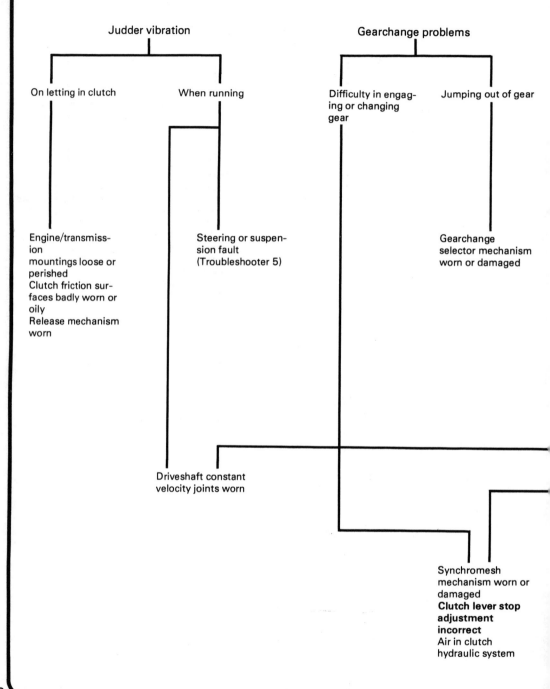

Judder vibration

On letting in clutch

When running

Engine/transmiss-
ion
mountings loose or
perished
Clutch friction sur-
faces badly worn or
oily
Release mechanism
worn

Steering or suspen-
sion fault
(Troubleshooter 5)

Driveshaft constant
velocity joints worn

Gearchange problems

Difficulty in engag-
ing or changing
gear

Jumping out of gear

Gearchange
selector mechanism
worn or damaged

Synchromesh
mechanism worn or
damaged
**Clutch lever stop
adjustment
incorrect**
Air in clutch
hydraulic system

CLUTCH & TRANSMISSION

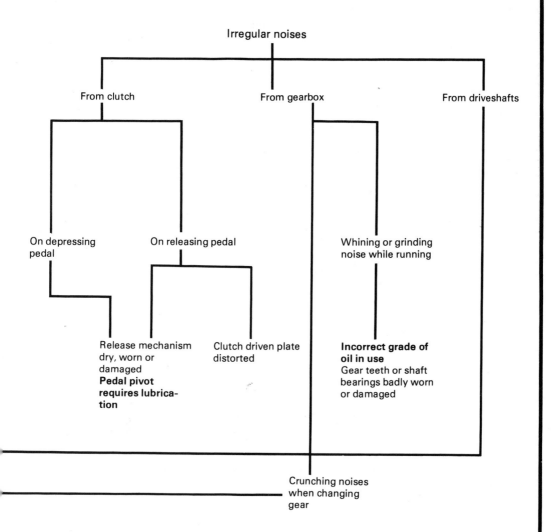

Irregular noises

From clutch

From gearbox

From driveshafts

On depressing pedal

On releasing pedal

Whining or grinding noise while running

Release mechanism dry, worn or damaged
Pedal pivot requires lubrication

Clutch driven plate distorted

Incorrect grade of oil in use
Gear teeth or shaft bearings badly worn or damaged

Crunching noises when changing gear

TROUBLESHOOTER 4:

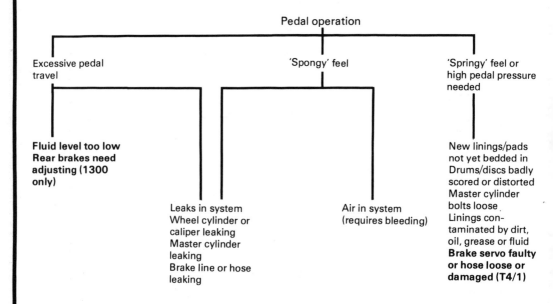

Pedal operation

Excessive pedal travel

**Fluid level too low
Rear brakes need adjusting (1300 only)**

Leaks in system
Wheel cylinder or caliper leaking
Master cylinder leaking
Brake line or hose leaking

'Spongy' feel

Air in system
(requires bleeding)

'Springy' feel or high pedal pressure needed

New linings/pads not yet bedded in
Drums/discs badly scored or distorted
Master cylinder bolts loose
Linings contaminated by dirt, oil, grease or fluid
Brake servo faulty or hose loose or damaged (T4/1)

TROUBLESHOOTER 5:

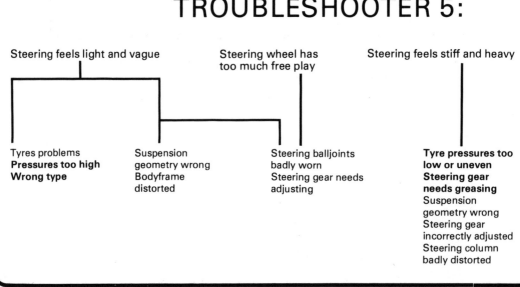

Steering feels light and vague

Steering wheel has too much free play

Steering feels stiff and heavy

Tyres problems
**Pressures too high
Wrong type**

Suspension geometry wrong
Bodyframe distorted

Steering balljoints badly worn
Steering gear needs adjusting

**Tyre pressures too low or uneven
Steering gear needs greasing**
Suspension geometry wrong
Steering gear incorrectly adjusted
Steering column badly distorted

BRAKES

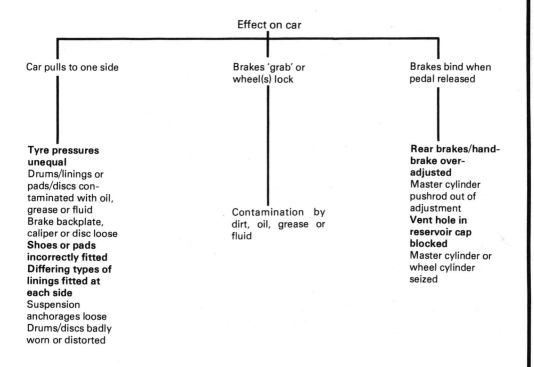

Effect on car

Car pulls to one side	Brakes 'grab' or wheel(s) lock	Brakes bind when pedal released
Tyre pressures unequal Drums/linings or pads/discs contaminated with oil, grease or fluid Brake backplate, caliper or disc loose **Shoes or pads incorrectly fitted** **Differing types of linings fitted at each side** Suspension anchorages loose Drums/discs badly worn or distorted	Contamination by dirt, oil, grease or fluid	**Rear brakes/hand-brake over-adjusted** Master cylinder pushrod out of adjustment **Vent hole in reservoir cap blocked** Master cylinder or wheel cylinder seized

STEERING & SUSPENSION

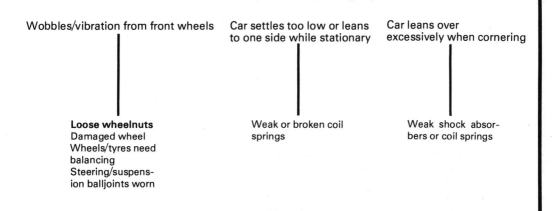

Wobbles/vibration from front wheels	Car settles too low or leans to one side while stationary	Car leans over excessively when cornering
Loose wheelnuts Damaged wheel Wheels/tyres need balancing Steering/suspension balljoints worn	Weak or broken coil springs	Weak shock absorbers or coil springs

TROUBLESHOOTER 6:

A fault occurring in any other electrical equipment or accessory not specifically referred to can usually be traced to one of three main causes, ie blown fuse; loose or broken connection to power supply or earth; or internal fault in the component concerned.

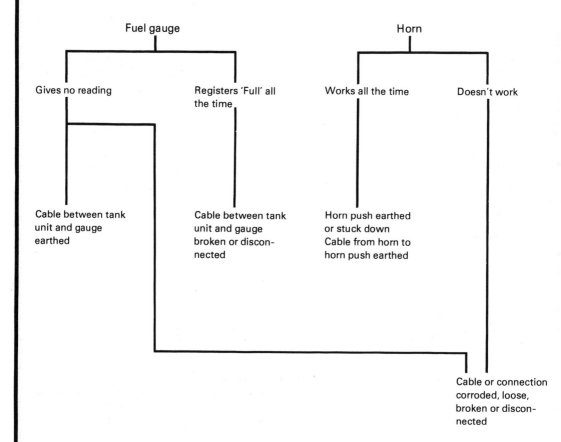

NOTE: This chart assumes that the battery installed in your car is in good condition and is of the correct specification, and that the terminal connections are clean and tight. A car used frequently for stop-start motoring or for short journeys (particularly in winter when lights, heater blower etc are likely to be in use) may need its battery recharged at intervals to keep it serviceable. If an electrical problem occurs, don't immediately suspect the starter or any other component without first checking that the battery is capable of supplying its demands!

ELECTRICS

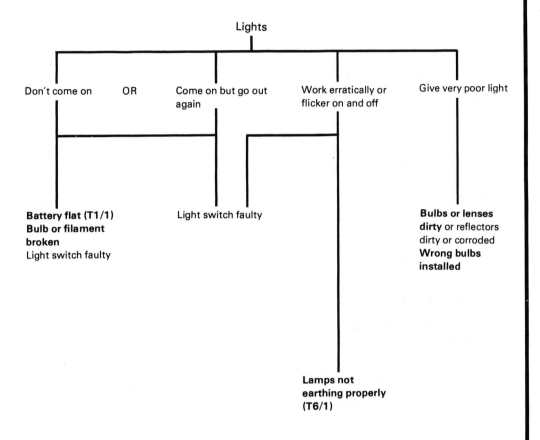

Lights

Don't come on   OR   Come on but go out
again

Work erratically or
flicker on and off

Give very poor light

Battery flat (T1/1)
Bulb or filament
broken
Light switch faulty

Light switch faulty

Bulbs or lenses
dirty or reflectors
dirty or corroded
Wrong bulbs
installed

Lamps not
earthing properly
(T6/1)

CROSS-REFERENCE TABLE

TROUBLESHOOTER REFERENCE	ADDITIONAL INFORMATION
T1/1	Either charge the battery from a battery charger, or use jump leads to start the car from another battery; make sure that the lead polarities are correct in both cases or you may do permanent damage, particularly if your car has an alternator.
T1/2	If the lead's loose, disconnect the battery earth lead then tighten the connection on the starter motor; make sure that the bolt doesn't turn while you're tightening the nut. Reconnect the battery earth lead.
T1/3	You can use a spanner on the square-ended shaft on the end of the starter motor. By turning it you'll normally be able to free it from the flywheel ring gear.
T1/4	Make sure all the connections are tight, then wipe the leads clean and dry with a lint-free cloth. Use an ignition system waterproofer (eg WD40 or Damp Start) to prevent problems in the future.
T1/5	An ignition coil or condenser is a simple item to fit, but make a note of the connections before removing them, and ensure that the coil's is the correct type. Renewal of the condenser is also straight-forward.
T1/6	To check the operation of the pump, detach the fuel outlet pipe (that's the one that goes to the carburettor) and operate it manually (if a mechanical pump) with the small lever on the side if there is one. If there's no lever, turn the engine over on the starter a few times. In either case there should be a steady stream of petrol if the pump's working properly. Cleaning the fuel pump filter is covered in the 12 000 mile Service Schedule.
T1/7	It's easy enough to tighten the attachment bolts if you've got a box or socket spanner of

TROUBLESHOOTER REFERENCE	ADDITIONAL INFORMATION
	the right size; if you haven't, it's not really a D-I-Y job.
T1/8	For a temporary repair a leaking hose can normally be bound up with adhesive tape or, better still, with a hose bandage available for this purpose.
T1/9	Wait till the system's cooled down, then top it up. If it happens a second time, get it looked at straight away or you could ruin your engine (if it hasn't happened already). If it's just a leaking hose you can probably bind it up as in T1/8 (above) to get yourself home.
T2/1	See T1/9.
T2/2	Driving carefully will probably get you home. An air line on the radiator core will clean out the dirt that's accumulated; if it's blocked internally, use a proprietary flushing compound.
T2/3	You may be able to repair the hose temporarily (see T1/8) but it'll almost certainly mean a new one.
T2/4	Drive more slowly – but without labouring the engine.
T4/1	Provided there's no loss of hydraulic fluid, you'll need a little extra pedal effort for braking but that's all. It may be possible to temporarily repair the hose as in T1/8.
T6/1	Remove the lamp lenses (see *In An Emergency*) and check for signs of rust. Where there's rust, scrape it off and apply a little petroleum jelly. Ensure that the screws securing the lamp body to the car are making good contact.

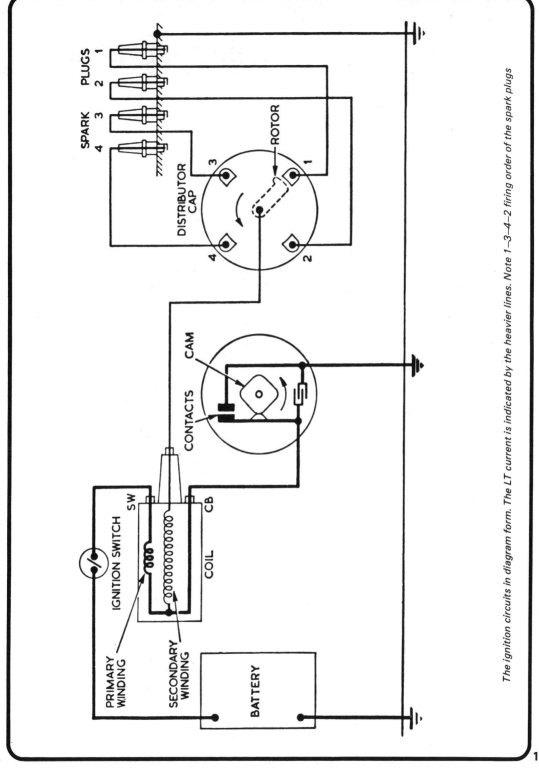

The ignition circuits in diagram form. The LT current is indicated by the heavier lines. Note 1–3–4–2 firing order of the spark plugs

CONVERSION

Distance

Inches (in)	X 25.400	=	Millimetres (mm)
Feet (ft)	X 0.305	=	Metres (m)
Miles	X 1.609	=	Kilometres (km)
Millimetres (mm)	X 0.039	=	Inches (in)
Metres (m)	X 3.281	=	Feet (ft)
Kilometres (km)	X 0.621	=	Miles

Capacity

Inches, cubic (cu in/in^3)	X 16.387	=	Centimetres, cubic (cc/cm^3)
Fluid ounce, imperial (fl oz)	X 35.51	=	Centimetres, cubic (cc/cm^3)
Fluid ounce, US (fl oz)	X 29.57	=	Centimetres, cubic (cc/cm^3)
Pints, imperial (imp pt)	X 0.568	=	Litres (L)
Quarts, imperial (imp qt)	X 1.1365	=	Litres (L)
Quarts, imperial (imp qt)	X 1.201	=	Quart, US (US qt)
Quarts, US (US qt)	X 0.9463	=	Litres (L)
Quarts, US (US qt)	X 0.8326	=	Quarts, imperial (imp qt)
Gallons, imperial (imp gal)	X 4.546	=	Litres (L)
Gallons, imperial (imp gal)	X 1.201	=	Gallons, US (US gal)
Gallons, US (US gal)	X 3.7853	=	Litres (L)
Gallons, US (US gal)	X 0.8326	=	Gallons, imperial (imp gal)
Centimetres, cubic (cc/cm^3)	X 0.061	=	Inches, cubic (cu in/in^3)
Centimetres, cubic (cc/cm^3)	X 0.02816	=	Fluid ounces, imperial (fl oz)
Centimeters, cubic (cc/cm^3)	X 0.03381	=	Fluid ounces, US (fl oz)
Litres (L)	X 28.16	=	Fluid ounces, imperial (fl oz)
Litres (L)	X 33.81	=	Fluid ounces, US (fl oz)
Litres (L)	X 1.760	=	Pints, imperial (imp pt)
Litres (L)	X 0.8799	=	Quarts, imperial (imp qt)
Litres (L)	X 1.0567	=	Quarts, US (US qt)
Litres (L)	X 0.220	=	Gallons, imperial (imp gal)
Litres (L)	X 0.264	=	Gallons, US (US gal)

Area

Inches, square (in^2/sq in)	X 645.160	=	Millimetres, square (mm^2/sq mm)
Feet, square (ft^2/sq ft)	X 0.093	=	Metres, square (m^2/sq m)
Millimetres, square (mm^2/sq mm)	X 0.002	=	Inches, square (in^2/sq in)
Metres, square (m^2/sq m)	X 10.764	=	Feet square (ft^2/sq ft)

Weight

Ounces (oz)	X 28.350	=	Grammes (g)
Pounds (lbs)	X 0.454	=	Kilogrammes (kg)
Grammes (g)	X 0.035	=	Ounces (oz)
Kilogrammes (kg)	X 2.205	=	Pounds (lbs)
Kilogrammes (kg)	X 35.274	=	Ounces (oz)

FACTORS

Pressure

Pounds/sq in (psi/lb/sq in/ lb/in^2)	X 0.070	= Kilogrammes/sq cm (kg/sq cm)
Pounds/sq in (psi/lb/sq in/ lb/in^2)	X 0.068	= Atmospheres (atm)
Kilogrammes sq cm (kg/sq cm)	X 14.223	= Pounds/sq in (psi/lb/sq in/ lb/in^2)
Atmospheres (atm)	X 14.696	= Pounds/sq in (psi/lb/sq in/ lb/in^2)

Torque

Pound - inches (lbf in)	X 0.0115	= Kilogramme - metres (kgf m)
Pound - inches (lbf in)	X 0.0833	= Pound - feet (lbf ft)
Pound - feet (lbf ft)	X 12	= Pound - inches (lbf in)
Pound - feet (lbf ft)	X 0.138	= Kilogramme - metres (kgf m)
Pound - feet (lbf ft)	X 1.356	= Newton - metres (Nm)
Kilogramme - metres (kgf m)	X 86.796	= Pound - inches (lbf in)
Kilogramme - metres (kgf m)	X 7.233	= Pound - feet (lbf ft)
Newton - metres (Nm)	X. 0.738	= Pound - feet (lbf ft)
Newton - metres (Nm)	X 0.102	= Kilogramme - metres (kgf m)

Speed

Miles - hour (mph)	X 1.609	= Kilometres - hour (kph)
Feet - second	X 0.305	= Metres - second (m/s)
Kilometres - hour (kph)	X 0.621	= Miles - hour (mph)
Metres - second (m/s)	X 3.281	= Feet - second
Metres - second (m/s)	X 3.600	= Kilometres - hour (kph)

Consumption

Miles - gallon, imperial (mpg)	X 0.354	= Kilometres - litre (km/l)
Kilometres - litre (km/l)	X 2.825	= Miles - gallon, imperial (mpg)

Temperature

Centigrade (^{o}C) to Fahrenheit (^{o}F)

$$\frac{9}{5}\,^{o}C + 32 = \,^{o}F$$

Fahrenheit (^{o}F) to Centigrade (^{o}C)

$$\frac{5}{9}(^{o}F - 32) = \,^{o}C$$

Index

109

Printed by
Haynes Publishing Group
Sparkford Yeovil Somerset
England